HOW CAN I HELP YOU?

HOW CAN I HELP YOU?

Basic Helping Skills for Christians

David J. Pope

LUMINARE PRESS
WWW.LUMINAREPRESS.COM

How Can I Help You?: Basic Helping Skills for Christians
Copyright © 2024 by David J. Pope

All rights reserved. This book or any portion thereof may not be reproduced or used in any manner whatsoever without the express written permission of the publisher, except for the use of brief quotations in a book review.

Printed in the United States of America

Luminare Press
442 Charnelton St.
Eugene, OR 97401
www.luminarepress.com

LCCN: 2024906554
ISBN: 979-8-88679-536-3

*In memory of my good friend
and former colleague, Owen Wengert.*

TABLE OF CONTENTS

Foreword ix
Introduction 1

   The Basics of Helping 3
   Addictions 15
   Codependency 36
   Anger 44
   Marital/Family Issues 53
   Trauma 68
   Shame vs. Guilt 75
   Depression/Anxiety 81
   Grief 91
   Other Mental Health Issues 99
   Disabilities 119
   Final Thoughts 129

Pope-isms 145
Acknowledgments 151
References 152
About the Author 155

Foreword

I was starting my own recovery journey when I first met Dave Pope, in the fall of 2014. We were attending a Celebrate Recovery meeting in Prescott, Arizona. After the large meeting disbanded and the men went into their open share meeting, Dave and I came into contact. As we went around the circle of men, offering our thoughts about the message and what we were struggling with, he introduced himself, stating he had just relocated from Nebraska. Dave had been in Celebrate Recovery there for several years and worked as a licensed therapist. He had come to Arizona to continue his career and eventually retire. Although I was new to recovery, I could tell Dave had a lot of recovery experience and knowledge as he shared.

Dave hadn't been attending our meetings for long before he was asked to teach one of the bi-weekly CR lessons. His rational, common sense and humorous approach to teaching was appreciated and he soon joined the leadership team. His years working in the addiction and mental health fields gave him many pearls of wisdom, which Dave freely shared. Now retired but still a leader in our CR, Dave has amassed a wealth of personal stories and practical applications for anyone who has a desire to help others struggling with issues of life from a Christian perspective. In addition to chemical addictions, this includes co-dependency, trauma, anger, marital situations, shame vs. guilt, mental health issues, physical disabilities, and more. Dave openly offers lessons he has learned as well as his own life experiences. He has many witty sayings that have come to be known as "Pope-isms." These phrases Dave recites from memory as he teaches at our CR meeting or leads our men's open share group.

Since Dave and I first met, I have become the ministry leader of that same CR group, and I am now Dave's sponsor. I heartily endorse what Dave has compiled in *How Can I Help You?* It is an enjoyable read that offers so much to anyone looking for basic instruction in helping others!

Dale Sams
Celebrate Recovery Ministry Leader, Prescott, AZ

Introduction

For those grammar experts out there thinking, "Shouldn't that be 'How *may* I help you?'" let me reassure you. I am not trying to address the question a helper asks a person in need, but rather the question a potential helper asks themselves: "How can *I* help *you*?" The Bible makes it very clear we are to help others. From Jesus's parable of the good Samaritan to the admonition in Galatians 6:2 "Bear one another's burdens, and so fulfill the law of Christ," the call to help each other is an expectation of all Christians.

But that doesn't mean that providing help to others is an easy or straightforward task. Many of us feel unsure of ourselves, unprepared to meet the needs of others and unskilled in dealing with challenging issues. Even the most willing helper may often ask "What can I do to help this person?"

In a forty-year career in addiction and mental health therapy I've encountered a myriad of complex issues facing a wide range of people, and have discovered, through many failures and some success, principles important to the work of helping others. I hope to share these with you in order to aid you in serving others in need.

Of course, I don't intend to turn anyone into a seasoned therapist just by reading a single book, but there are some simple techniques that I and others have found useful. I'll also provide a wealth of analogies and examples that might be helpful in situations you encounter. There will be several scripture references as well (taken from the New King James Version), with attempts to apply biblical instructions and principles to current day issues.

HOW THIS BOOK IS ARRANGED

The first chapter will give some basic standards regarding helping others, with important considerations for anyone trying to aid those in need. A list of DOs and DON'Ts will be included in this and all other chapters. The next ten chapters will address some of the most common and challenging issues facing others, in and out of the Church, along with a few specific suggestions on simple actions that you can take right now. Each of these chapters will contain a definition of the issue, a synopsis of the work individuals need to do to address their problems themselves, and ways you can aid them in that process. The chapter on disabilities will include my wife's story about her disability and her observations on how to aid others with special needs. Finally, over the years I've collected a long list of quotes and quips a coworker came to label "Pope-isms." The vast majority of these did not originate with me, and some I have no idea of the origin, but I've given credit to the source where I was able to find such.

If you have a heart to serve others, you have embraced a worthy cause. May you be filled with confidence and God's love as you do so, and it would be a great honor if anything in this book can aid you in that endeavor.

Chapter One

THE BASICS OF HELPING

If you've ever had people come up to you saying, "I just don't know what to do!", "I'm at my wit's end!", "I've tried everything", or "I knew I could talk to you—you'll know just what to do", then you have probably felt some apprehension about your ability to give others the help they desperately seek. How do you help a friend whose child has been caught using meth? How do you comfort a neighbor whose spouse has just died? While the Bible doesn't give you specific instruction on just what to say in these situations, there are principles in scripture and techniques in counseling that can be helpful guides in aiding others.

I THINK THE MOST IMPORTANT INITIAL CONSIDERATION is to know where the person is in addressing the problem so far. Proverbs 20:5 states, "Counsel in the heart of man is like deep water, but a man of understanding will draw it out." The person seeking your help has probably already tried several things themselves in search of a way out of their quandary; hear them out about their journey thus far. Taking the time to hear someone's story will help you understand how they came to be in their current circumstances. You'll also be able to build your relationship with the person you're hoping to help. I've built some of my most cherished friendships by helping others or having them help me through my personal struggles. This, I believe, is part of the groundwork involved in "bearing each other's burdens" (Galatians 6:2).

THE PROBLEM-SOLVING MODEL

There is a five-step, problem-solving model I discovered long ago that can be helpful as a starting point.

> 1. Gather information.
> An old adage is "a problem accurately diagnosed is 85 percent solved." We need to know what we're dealing with before we can look at what to do about it. Ask questions like "When did the problem start?", "Who is it impacting?", "What have you tried so far?", "How does the problem manifest itself?", "Are there times the problem **doesn't** occur?", etc. Act like a news reporter just gathering facts. Resist the urge to solve the issue until you've collected all the information you can. Many solutions will emerge simply by taking a broader perspective and looking at what you're dealing with. An example of this occurred in a small town's debate about whether or not to purchase some double-decker buses from England to promote tourism. Amid the debate, one person pointed out the steering wheel is on the opposite side in English buses, making them too expensive to renovate for use in the United States. If the investigation about the issue had uncovered this fact initially, the debate could have been solved immediately.

2. Brainstorm possible responses.

Without making any judgment about the efficacy of a response, think of all the possible responses to address the issue at hand. Be sure to include "Do Nothing," as this is the default option if you don't choose something else. Honestly, sometimes the best thing you can do in a problematic situation is nothing. Investigating available resources is an important part of this step. What tools, programs, success stories or support sources do you have at your disposal? A hypothetical example: If your problem is being unemployed, possible responses could be: choosing to be homeless, committing a robbery, moving back in with your parents, submitting twenty applications a day, standing on a street corner with a sign, etc. While many of the responses will immediately be seen as ridiculous, by allowing the brainstorming process to sweep with a wide brush, you will take glimpses outside the box you may feel trapped in, discovering potential solutions you haven't thought of. I'd recommend, in most situations, looking at no fewer than seven options and no more than twenty-five before considering the potential benefits of each.

3. Assess pros and cons.

This is the point at which a potential helper can be most useful, thinking through the likely outcome of various responses to problems. Another adage is, "If you keep doing what you're doing you'll keep getting what you got." Remember the joke about the guy who goes to the doctor and says, "Doc, it hurts when I raise my hand over my head." The doctor responds, "Then stop raising your hand over your head." If what the person is doing isn't making things better, help them admit it. If a particular option has worked well for you or others, you can suggest they give it a try. There may be a response they've tried in the past that would be worth trying now. It's possible the person you're trying to help has been responding in ways that are actually making things worse or causing other issues; telling the person so in objective, nonjudgmental terms may be crucial to their healing. Even the most extreme responses may have some level of validity when you consider the potential impact.

4. Choose, and DO IT!
How many times have you known the answer to a problem but failed to follow through on it? You're going to stay in the hole you're in until you do the work of getting out. I have a lot to say on the importance of accountability in later chapters. Simply stated, checking to make sure a person has followed through on what they've agreed to do may be the difference between success or failure for someone dealing with a difficult problem. I've had many people respond to challenges to change their behavior with, "Okay, I'll try." I give them the Yoda response: "Try not. Do, or do not. There is no try." Admonish the person to put forth the action and accept the outcome. Of course, the response that's chosen may not actually be successful (as will be addressed in the final step), so a period of trial and error may be needed.

5. Evaluate.

There's a humorous sign I saw that read, "The beatings will continue until morale improves." You may be working hard at a solution that just isn't having the positive effect you had intended. If the solution isn't working, it's time to recommend the person you're helping try something else. Also, the solution may have produced unplanned side effects, which now need to be addressed. As Jesus became more popular, it became more difficult for Him to move about and speak to the people. His solution? He climbed a hill, resulting in the famous Sermon on the Mount, and spoke from a boat to people on the shore, so his voice could carry. The process of evaluation will also help in staying focused on the solution rather than on the problem.

EXAMPLE VS. MORALIZING

One of the most effective group exercises I've used to indicate the power of example is this: I make an "OK" sign with my finger and thumb, then instruct the group to make the same sign. I then say "now put it on your chin" while at the same time putting it on my cheek. Most people will put the circle on their cheek. Even those that do put it on their chin, as instructed, will hesitate, trying to resolve the conflict between what they see and what they heard. If your example doesn't match your word, you've cheapened the value of your word. James 1:22 states, "But be doers of the word, and not hearers only, deceiving yourselves."

While I understand the need to point out sinful behavior when you see it, many fail to regard the "restore him gently" part of the instructions in Galatians 6:1. Your grandmother probably told you, "You can catch more flies with honey than you can with vinegar." By focusing on an effective response to an issue and being supportive, your ability to be helpful will be aided. If you're helping someone through a problem you yourself have addressed successfully, think of how others patiently supported you (or how you wished they would have) and show the same patience with the person in need.

TYPES OF HELP

One of the most useful lessons I received during my training for a Master's of Christian Counseling degree had to do with the importance of knowing at what level to offer help to others. In general, there are four levels of help: 1) Office care, done by counselors or church staff working in an official capacity. Unless you have specific training, don't try to provide this level of care, but seek out those that have such training; 2) Sermon care, done by preachers or teachers speaking on a specific topic in a group format to address an issue one or more people are dealing with. If you're in a position to preach or teach, think about how you can be most helpful to those in your audience through your presentations; 3) Friend care, done by any of us with a person in need we have built a relationship with; and 4) Schmooze care, checking in regularly with people, in an informal manner, about the issues they're dealing with. This can be very effective, especially if you go beyond simply asking, "How Are You Doing?" to really expressing concern and empathy.

Understand, please, that our role as helpers is not to fix people; let's let Jesus do the fixing. Our job is to provide support and express concern. People in need must do their own work in solving the problems they face and making the changes they need to make in their own lives. My philosophy is, give a man a fish, you feed him for a day. Teach a man to fish, you feed him for his life. Give him a fish every day, he'll forget how to fish. There are people that will try to use your good intentions to be helpful to get you to do things for them; resist such appeals by asking the person what they intend to do for themselves, then ask how you can hold them accountable for doing so.

I learned a valuable lesson along this line at a training course on how to counsel others in just a few sessions. They emphasized the importance of knowing what a person you are trying to help is a "customer" for. Imagine going to a department store for a coat and the clerk tries to sell you gloves instead—you're not going to stay at that store very long. A person may be coming to you for help with their marriage though it is obvious to you they also have an alcohol problem. You won't be able to address their alcohol problem unless they're confident you will attend to their marriage issue. One of the things you learn to do in the addiction field is help people with issues they don't really think are much of a problem. By working with them to discover the areas where they do see a need for help, I was able to show them a broader world of interplay between what they were initially a customer for and what they truly need to address to get to where they need to be. It's like telling the person coming in for a coat that they'd be a lot warmer if they got a pair of gloves also.

DON'T OUTRUN YOUR HEADLIGHTS

A recovery sponsor I had for many years (may he rest in peace) drilled into my head the principle of not outrunning your headlights, in other words not going beyond your knowledge or capacity. In helping others, you can find yourself in a lot of trouble by trying to help with an issue beyond your ability. When the apostles encountered a demon-possessed person they could not heal (Matthew 17), they went to Jesus for help. One of the smartest things you can do is recognize what you don't know. I have always had others I can go to for advice or input; they've been able to help me avoid many missteps through their guidance.

It's a good idea to know about resources for Christian mental health therapy, for addiction and marital counseling and who can provide quality professional help on a sliding scale. It's valuable to investigate which professionals a person in need may have utilized already and determine if your suggestions match up with what those professionals are telling them. If you find yourself embroiled in a highly emotional issue beyond your capacity, don't be embarrassed to say so—seek support sooner rather than later. Keeping the confidence of the person you're helping is, of course, an important consideration, so make sure that person knows when you seek input from others.

FOUR STEPS TO CHANGE

There are four steps that must be completed in order to change from an unhealthy behavior pattern to a good one. It is important to know which step a person seeking help is in.

1. Know when you're doing it wrong. *The Living Bible* paraphrase renders Jeremiah 6:14 as "You can't heal a wound by pretending it's not there." The first step in change is to recognize the problem for what it is. Admitting when you do something wrong is a prerequisite to doing it better next time.

2. When you do it wrong, correct it right away. I'll be reviewing the 12 steps later in the addiction chapter; Step 10 of the 12 steps instructs us to continually examine ourselves and, when wrong, promptly correct it.

3. Do it right more often. After we become proficient in recognizing when we're doing wrong and fixing it promptly, it's time to start catching ourselves **before** we do the wrong thing. I believe keeping track of successes is more motivating than just keeping track of failures.

4. Do it right consistently. Though we won't likely be perfect in ending all bad behavior, we can reach a point where bad behavior is no longer our norm and our natural tendency is to make the right choice. I've heard that if you do the same behavior nineteen times in a row your brain will construct a pathway from the start of the behavior to the end of it, so it's easier to do the behavior without thinking about it. If you doubt this, look at which shoe you tend to put on first, then try to put on the other shoe first tomorrow. It will take an enormous amount of concentration to change your unconscious patterns. While that's obviously a burden when the behavior is destructive, it's a blessing when we develop healthy disciplines.

DOs and DON'Ts

DO pray before and during the helping process. I take a broad view of James 5:16 "The effective, fervent prayer of a righteous man avails much." Having a connection with God is the best mindset to start with in serving others.

DO remain patient, calm, and steady. When working at a group home with very troubled teen girls it was made crystal clear that we, as staff, were to be the solid object in a river of turmoil. The parable about the house built on the rock applies when helping others. Your care and love for others doesn't require you to match their level of panic or woe.

DO take care of yourself. My mother (may she rest in peace) would often make herself stressed worrying about someone else's issues. It's harder to help others if you take on their problems. I have often been asked, in my profession as a therapist, "Don't you have trouble taking people's problems home with you?" My response is, "I don't take them to the parking lot." I call it professional jadedness. It's not that I don't care; I just realize my stressing about someone else's issues isn't going to help them and can only harm me. Your own peace and contentment are a prerequisite to helping others find their own peace.

DO seek support when needed. You're not going to have all the answers and when we need help ourselves, we need to seek it. I can't count the number of times someone has come to me for help with an issue I too was in the process of dealing with. It seems to me these occasions are serendipitous, God giving both of us a chance to help each other and seek mutually supportive solutions.

DO be the best example you can be. A genuine, conscientious Christian can help many people simply by living a

Godly life and being a model for others. It is said, "Preach the Gospel at all times; when necessary, use words."

DON'T condemn. You can admonish someone without being their judge. Focus on the behavior and its consequences, not the person and their flaws. Look at how gentle Jesus was with repentant sinners, as opposed to his harsh statements about the behavior of the religious leaders. I have been blessed with the ability to see the good in every person I've dealt with professionally (murderers, child molesters, sociopaths, etc.). While their behaviors are often abhorrent, as many of our sinful behaviors are, all people are creations of God and have the capacity for repentance and redemption if they seek it.

DON'T go beyond your relationship with the person in need. The saying is, "No one cares how much you know until they know how much you care." Examine your motives; if you see you're seeking personal credit or approval rather than acting out of a true desire to be of service, it might be time to back off.

DON'T give up! Change is a marathon, not a sprint, so don't quit while the process is still going on. This doesn't mean keep doing things that aren't working but keep striving to be of aid to others when possible. Don't be discouraged if the person you're helping has a setback or becomes embroiled in the same issue again. Stay in the battle and celebrate the victories whenever they occur.

DON'T push! Unsolicited advice is usually perceived as criticism. It's okay to ask if you can help someone; but, if the offer is declined, accept their decision. You're not in a position to force anyone to be who you think they should be even if you believe you have justification for calling them out. Matthew 18 has a great guide on how to address those in sin who reject admonition.

DON'T miss the chance to build friendships. While the focus will be on the problem during the helping process, bonding with one another is a blessed byproduct of these encounters.

Chapter Two

ADDICTIONS

Virtually everyone over the age of five has experienced or heard of addiction. There are many definitions, but the one I have used for many decades comes from Robert and Mary McAuliffe. In their book *The Essentials of Chemical Dependency* (1975), they outline the most succinct, useful definition of addiction I've ever heard: addiction is **an unhealthy relationship to a drug in expectation of a reward**. There are three considerations in this model:

1. A Reward
People become addicted to drugs because they like what the drug does to/for them. While this may seem obvious, understand that many people **don't** like the way drugs feel. I loved the way marijuana felt from the first time I tried it and couldn't wait to do it again. One of my brothers, on the other hand, hated how it felt. I developed an addiction while he did not. Liking the way a drug feels doesn't necessarily make you an addict, but it surely makes you a **potential** addict.

2. A Relationship
This doesn't necessarily mean using a drug every day (although using every day is an indication of a

strong relationship). It means the drug has taken on a significant place in your life; you've come to rely on it. I may like the way lemonade tastes and that may not be an issue, but if I'm devoting a significant part of my income to lemonade—if I'm avoiding friends that don't drink lemonade—if I'm spending increasing amounts of time securing my supply of lemonade—if I wake up each morning longing for my first glass of lemonade of the day, I probably need to take a look at my lemonade problem.

3. The Relationship Has Become Unhealthy.
This is the one addicts fight about the most. There's a T-shirt that says, "I don't have a drinking problem. I drink, I fall down, I get up—no problem." It's not necessary to contest whether the reward is worth the unhealthy outcome; if the unhealthy aspects are present because of the drug relationship, you qualify as an addict. Of course, anyone on blood pressure medicine can acknowledge it is possible to have a healthy relationship with a drug, but a person that likes how a drug feels is less objective in determining how damaging the relationship has become than those around them. If a person isn't sure how much the drug relationship has become unhealthy, they can ask those around them; the ones that care most about a person and aren't themselves caught up in the same addiction will likely give a more objective assessment. There's a saying that if one person tells you that you have a tail, they're probably crazy. If twelve people in a row tell you that you have a tail, look behind you.

The McAuliffes also outline the progression addiction takes through four stages. To paraphrase:

The Pleasure Stage. Think of the teenager that is just starting to drink a few beers or smoke some weed at parties and really enjoys the way it feels, how it makes them have more fun with friends. Sure, it might be against the law, they must hide it from their parents, and they throw up if they drink too much, but wow! It feels good to be high and they can't wait to do it again. They have developed an unhealthy relationship with the drugs and are in the initial stages of addiction.

The Relief Stage. Think about a relationship with a person—initially you just interact with them to have a good time, but gradually you start to rely on them to make you feel better when you're down and expect them to help you deal with emotional issues. In this stage of the drug relationship, the addict begins using it to relax, to make it easier to talk to people, to overcome depression or other emotional issues, to forget about traumatic issues from the past. The relationship has become stronger and the unhealthy consequences the addict is willing to sustain have increased.

The Maintenance Stage. At this point, the addict is going steady with the drug. Alcohol is on the grocery list every week and the budget accounts for it. The bartender doesn't even need to turn around at five o'clock—he puts a beer in front of the addict's usual spot because he knows they'll be there like clockwork. The drug dealer sets aside the addict's weekly supply every Saturday because he knows the addict will be there for the purchase; if he isn't, he assumes the addict is in jail or dead. One client I worked with had bought a bottle of alcohol every day from the same convenience store for years. After sobering up for several months, the client happened to go into the store to buy a pack of cigarettes and the cashier shouted, "It's a miracle—you're alive!" The cashier had seriously assumed that only a catastrophe could have kept this person from buying his daily supply. In this stage, life accommodates the addiction rather than the addiction fitting in with other life needs. It's not that you **can't** live without it, but that you **don't** live without it. The biggest test is to try going without it for a few weeks. How different does your life become? How much of a loss do you feel without it? Do you experience the same grief as when a committed relationship with a person ends?

The Oblivion Stage. People can stay in the maintenance stage for many years, but eventually the addiction will catch up with them. They'll experience financial trouble, family trouble, physical trouble or (what I usually saw in my profession) legal trouble, and they'll come to the realization they can't keep going like this without some major consequences. Some people see their first major consequence and quit forever. While that seems like a logical move, the draw of the addiction usually causes addicts to reject this option. Some continue to try to maintain their relationship with the drug, coming up with ideas of how to keep it under control, e.g., "I'll only drink on weekends.", "I'll only use speed when I need to study for school.", "I'll keep to a certain amount per day or week.", "I won't let it get out of hand." Even after repeated failures to keep to their self-prescribed limits, they continue to try to maintain the drug relationship with limited consequences. Some addicts reach the point of defeat and say to themselves, "I know I can't control it—so what? If it kills me or puts me in jail I don't care as long as I'm high." This group has entered the final, terminal stage of addiction and have submitted themselves to the oblivion the drug provides, regardless of the outcome.

There may be a tendency to think that the earlier stages are not that big a deal but make no mistake: addiction is not only progressive, it is irreversibly progressive. You can't go back to an earlier stage once you've advanced in the drug relationship. The principle at play is, you can't date your ex. If you get out of a bad relationship, you can't go back and date the person a few times and think you're going to keep the old problems from resurfacing. Even this scenario has a better chance than trying to keep an unhealthy drug relationship under control. A person can change, the drug never will. If I had the ability to keep people from enjoying the effects of drugs, I might be able to find a permanent cure. I'd also be a billionaire. The cure doesn't exist. If a person has developed an unhealthy relationship with a drug, the path of addiction is going to go downhill until they can sever the drug relationship and find a new, healthier way to receive the rewards sought from the drug.

OTHER ADDICTIONS

A preacher friend and I came to the conclusion that everyone is what he called "sin addicts." We are all drawn to that behavior we know goes against God's will but gives us some sort of pleasure/relief, and we find we can't consistently pull ourselves away from the behavior without God's help. The battle Paul describes in Romans 7, between his spiritual desire and his sinful nature, is a battle we can all relate to in some manner. While not everyone gets a good feeling from being high on a drug, there is likely some other behavior or source of sinful pleasure we've all fallen into. There's a reason why, in a time of stress, the alcoholic goes to the bar, the drug addict goes to the dealer, the porn addict goes to the internet, the gambler goes to the casino, the shopping addict goes to the mall, etc. Here's a brief list of some of the issues beyond alcohol/drug addiction that may embroil people in spiritual battles they can't seem to win.

Gambling. My definition of gambling addiction is "an unhealthy relationship to gambling, expecting a reward." That rush felt in the action of betting, the thrill of the win, and the desire to win back lost money overcomes the consequences: losing money you don't have, disappointing those impacted by your gambling, and embarrassment when the true extent of the relationship to gambling comes to light.

Pornography. My definition of pornography addiction is "an unhealthy relationship to porn, expecting a reward" (seeing a pattern?). I've heard that the two most common subjects of online searches are Christianity and pornography, likely often searched by the same person. Many otherwise Godly men have built a secret life of watching porn that keeps them from fully being who God wants them to be, and they're too embarrassed to ask for help.

Work Addictions. Even though work can be very rewarding, it's entirely possible a relationship with one's career can become unhealthy. Balancing work and home are a challenge in the best of circumstances, but if work efforts are pulling against the relationships with family and church, an addiction may have developed. I have had to tell overly demanding employers, "I have a personal asset and a business liability—my family comes first."

I could go on and on with potential addictions, such as video games, television, and social media. Suffice it to say, if your enjoyment of an activity or substance interferes with your ability to be who God wants you to be, it's time to take a hard look at yourself.

So how can we help those that have discovered they've developed an addiction?

ACCOUNTABILITY

The most important factor in helping someone recover from addiction is to be a source of accountability. I love it when people tell me how they recovered "on their own." I will ask such a person, "Didn't anyone know you were trying to change? Wasn't there anyone or anything that supported your decision to seek recovery?" Usually, people that say they did it on their own mean they didn't go to a formal recovery program. While there are many examples of people recovering without such programs, I've never met anyone that broke free of an addiction without the support of others. Let's face it, if people could just keep their addictive behavior under control through their own efforts there would be few addicts. I heard a former professional football player and speaker for the Fellowship of Christian Athletes say, in a big, booming voice, "You do not need to convince me that the Devil is a worthy foe. I've done battle with him myself. If you think you can beat him one-on-one, he's got you right where he wants you." This is not a battle we are intended to fight alone; we need to unite with and confide in our fellow warriors.

You've probably heard the term "sponsor" before. Here's my analogy for sponsorship: Let's say you wanted to climb Mt. Everest. I could be really supportive, get you the best climbing equipment, and find you the best books on climbing, but when you start climbing the mountain, you're on your own—I don't know how to climb Everest! You need a guide that's been up the mountain before and can help you climb. A sponsor in a 12-step program or other support group is someone that has personal success in the recovery process and a willingness to guide others in their recovery. Effective sponsors have a track record of personal success (over a year of personal recovery is recommended), practice principles of recovery themselves, and have the time to nurture someone new to the recovery process. Having the desire to give back what you've been given by those that have helped you is an important qualifier. I've seen people that try to build an empire of people they sponsor. A coworker, long ago, was proud to say he was sponsoring over forty people; another coworker said, "Come on, man—Jesus only sponsored twelve!" If you have had success in your own recovery, you possess a priceless gift that can be life-changing for someone trapped in an addiction. Even if you don't feel confident in being a sponsor, you can always be an accountability partner, or "climbing buddy." This involves mutual sharing of your successes and setbacks in dealing with your personal struggles and sharing of mutual concern with your accountability partner as you both progress on this spiritual journey.

MANY WELL-MEANING PEOPLE ARE AWARE OF OTHERS dealing with an addiction and have a desire to help them but have no real experience with that issue themselves. You can still agree to hold a person accountable by asking them if they're communicating with a sponsor or accountability partner, going to support groups, or following through with other commitments they've made. Investigating who in your congregation or personal circle has recovery experience may also be helpful even before you're asked to help an addict in need.

CELEBRATE RECOVERY

Before I get to Celebrate Recovery, let me give a quick history of 12-step programs in general. In 1935, in Akron, Ohio, the program of Alcoholics Anonymous was initiated by two alcoholics that had the idea that helping others with alcoholism would help them stay sober. An important event in the start of this program (described in the chapter "Bill's Story" in *Alcoholics Anonymous*, 4th Edition, 2020) was when one of the founders, Bill, sought the other founder, Dr. Bob, not for help himself, but with an offer to help Dr. Bob. I heard a trustee in A.A. state, "It's important to think of A.A. not as a 'self-help' program, but as a 'help others' program." There is no doubt A.A. is the largest, most effective recovery support program in history, with A.A. meetings in virtually every country around the globe and many millions of alcoholics finding freedom there. Many other separate recovery programs have developed from the success A.A. demonstrated, including Narcotics Anonymous, Gamblers Anonymous, Al-anon (for the friends and family of alcoholics), and a host of others.

A.A. has a 12-step program of recovery that members utilize to achieve sobriety and guide mutual support. I'll be giving a brief description of the 12 steps shortly but it's vital to know of A.A.'s non-religious stance and their concept of "God as you understand him." A.A. isn't connected with any church, denomination, religious philosophy, or organization. In a series of taped lectures I had the opportunity to listen to many years ago, the founder Bill described how important it is that newcomers to A.A. come to their own personal understanding of spirituality, however they choose to define it.

In 1992, a church leader at Saddleback Church in California went to their pastor Rick Warren (author of *The Purpose Driven Life*), with the idea of starting a recovery program for addicts that clearly focused on Jesus as their higher power and merged biblical principles with 12-step philosophy. The result was the inception of the Celebrate Recovery program, which has now grown to (as of February 2022) over 37,000 groups worldwide.

My personal recovery story began at age 17, when I was hospitalized with a toxic psychosis due to my use of a variety of drugs. I started to practice the 12 steps while attending multiple 12-step programs. While I was able to achieve success in sobriety (I've now been drug/alcohol free for over forty-five years) and developed a personal form of spirituality, I had a dilemma when I became a Christian in my late twenties. Some people in 12-step programs didn't adhere to the teachings of the Bible, often engaged in behaviors clearly not appropriate for Christians and, though the programs themselves state they have no opinion on outside issues, some members often disparaged those involved in organized religion. I chose to devote myself to the Church and broke from traditional 12-step programs. As a result, I struggled with inconsistent success against my addictive, sinful nature, until I began attending a congregation with a Celebrate Recovery group. It has been transformational—I am able to return to a regular practice of the 12 steps while incorporating biblical truths, with the support of others in the Church. Celebrate Recovery utilizes 8 principles that sort of mirror the 12 steps, with scriptural references related to each step/principle.

I'M NO EXPERT ON THE 12 STEPS; THERE IS NO SUCH thing in any official sense. But I've practiced and taught about the 12 steps and 8 principles for decades. Here's a brief overview of how they work:

> Step 1/Principle 1—In both Celebrate Recovery and 12-step programs the first step is to admit that you are powerless over your personal issue or addiction. Until an addict acknowledges that their sin problem is bigger than they can handle on their own, they're not likely to have any lasting success. Healing starts with an acknowledgment that, as Paul describes in Romans 7, we can't do what we know we should or avoid what we know we shouldn't without the transformational power God provides us. We also need to acknowledge that our lives have become unmanageable. My take on this is that everyone's life is unmanageable. None of us can make life go the way we want it to, and the sooner we accept that fact the sooner Christ can work with us. We are just pebbles on a vast beach. Each of us is an important part of the beach and the beach wouldn't be the same without us, but **we don't own the beach!** We're not here to get the other pebbles to submit to our will. We are here to cooperate with the creator and designer of the beach to be the pebble He designed us to be.
>
> Step2/Principle 2—Once an addict accepts that they can't control their tendency to go against God's will and that they can't control the world around them, now what? If there were only one step, this would be a depressing program! The good news is, this isn't where it ends, it's where it begins. A.A. and other such programs

ask, in the second step, that members come to believe in a higher power, without defining what or who that power is. In Celebrate Recovery, the second principle is to whole-heartedly believe that God exists and wants to help us in our recovery. We have to believe that God isn't just a detached, supreme being aloof from our needs but a loving father that cares about our struggles and has the power, as well as the desire, to heal us.

Step 3/Principle 3—After accepting our powerlessness and God's desire to help us, the next step is to make a commitment to God. In A.A. this means committing to the standards of the higher power we believe in; in Celebrate Recovery this involves wholly submitting all our life and our will to Christ and His will for us. Beyond obeying the Gospel and becoming a Christian, this involves giving Christ ultimate authority in all areas of our life. The analogy I use to explain the difference between steps 2 and 3 involves a tightrope walker that strung his tightrope across a waterfall and began walking across, first with a bar, then riding a bicycle, then pushing a wheelbarrow. A reporter voiced his amazement, and the tightrope walker asked, "Do you believe I can walk across that tightrope?" To which the reporter replied, "Sure, I believe it; I've seen you do it three times." The tightrope walker then said, "Great, get in the wheelbarrow—you're coming with me." Believing God **can** change us is one thing, putting our life fully in His hands is quite another. I had one person ask, "What if I turn myself over to God and He wants me to sell all I have and be a missionary in Iran?" My answer? If you truly believe that's where God wants you, start learning Farsi.

We must trust that the happiest and most functional we can be is when our will is most aligned with God's will.

Steps 4 & 5/Principle 4—You may wonder how a person will ever know what God's will is for them. The answer is, they'll have to do an inventory. Think of this as being under new management—you're going to want to do a thorough assessment; keep what works and get rid of what doesn't. There are many inventory guides out there to aid in this process; Celebrate Recovery has a detailed inventory guide and a thorough description of how to complete it. The two essential elements of a good inventory are **be fearless**, writing about all those things we're afraid to tell others, and **be thorough**, putting down everything pertinent. It is one of the greatest acts of self-discovery a person can ever do. Choosing who to share this inventory with is an important consideration. It should be someone that can be objective; a spouse, for example, isn't likely to hear all about the negative aspects of addiction without having an emotional response. It should also be someone that is able to share in the person's recovery journey after this step, as they will possess a great deal of knowledge about the person's history and can see old patterns reemerging.

Step 6 & 7/Principle 5—Now that an addict knows their assets and defects, it's time to make an agreement with God that they will change those aspects of their character that don't agree with His will. Romans 12:2 says it best: "And do not be conformed to this world, but be transformed by the renewing of your mind, that you may prove what is that good and acceptable and perfect will of God." Rather than simply focusing on our primary addiction, we seek to change everything that keeps us from being the people God envisions. Many people in Celebrate Recovery come in dealing with one issue, only to find a number of other issues they need to work on. This is growth! A famous Native American parable about seeking to change our defects to assets fits here: A grandfather said to his grandson, "Everyone has inside them two wolves, a good wolf, and a bad wolf. These two wolves fight continually for control of the person." The grandson asked, "Which one wins?" The answer: "Whichever one you feed." In this principle we commit to feeding the positive.

Step 8 & 9/Principles 6—The next step involves making amends, and, in the Celebrate Recovery principle, offering forgiveness to those that have hurt us. It's correcting the damage we've caused by our sinful, addictive behavior. One thing about making amends: it's not just saying I'm sorry, its mending damage. If I have a hole in a shirt, it does me no good to apologize to the shirt. I need to repair the hole. In the same way, apologizing to a store I shoplifted from means little if not accompanied by payment for what I took. Forgiveness is an area that has kept many people stuck—they just can't bring themselves to let go of the harm others have done to them. But remember, the goal is to set yourself free—the person that harmed you is still accountable to God, so part of this step is to let Him have your pain and trust Him to deal in His way with the person that harmed you.

Step 10 & 11/Principle 7—The final steps outline the continued recovery process. Every now and then people will tell me they've completed the 12 steps. Oh, really?

How do you complete "continued"? This is not a project to be completed but a direction of life to guide us to the end of our days. We are to admit when our behavior goes against God's will, make corrections promptly, utilize prayer and meditation, remain in God's word, and seek to continuously improve our understanding of what God wants for us. I heard of a preacher who's only prayer at night is "God, if you have anything for me to do tomorrow, wake me up." The idea is to align our day-to-day lives with God's plan, God's word, and God's love.

Step 12/Principle 8—The final step involves a commitment to live by these principles and aid others that struggle. The principle of helping others is at the core of the success all these programs have had. The basic text of Narcotics Anonymous states that "the therapeutic value of one addict helping another is without parallel." Having a heart to be of service is not only a benefit to the world around us, it is a primary principle in personal recovery.

One other important distinction about Celebrate Recovery: unlike other recovery support programs that focus their attention only on their primary issue, Celebrate Recovery is open to anyone. If you've never been, attending a few meetings will help you understand how this program can aid virtually any struggling Christian. You may also discover that you can be helped with any of your own struggles.

Aiding a Christian struggling with addictions will likely involve sharing your own efforts to change. It's a fun and rewarding exercise, sharing your experiences with others.

I believe the Church should operate more like Celebrate Recovery. If the Church looked more like a hospital for hurting sinners, it would be more attractive to those battling their own issues, many of whom are afraid "church people" won't understand. Celebrate Recovery is a place that is safe for everyone to open up, without judgment or condemnation. Wouldn't it be amazing if the Church as a whole were that way?

RELAPSE

I would love to tell you that every recovery story ends with "and they lived happily ever after with no more struggles with addiction," but sadly this is quite often not the case. Relapse does occur and the recovery process should prepare for such a risk. There are three stages of relapse: Prelapse, Lapse and Relapse.

Prelapse refers to the conditions that led to a weakening of the recovery resolve. Examples include: stopping support-group attendance, alienation from support sources, starting to associate with former unhealthy friends, slacking on spiritual disciplines and the like. Individually, any one of these setbacks can go unnoticed and may not have any serious consequences, but collectively they can erode the commitment to recovery and set in motion a slide back into active addiction. I compare this to a car going up a great big hill with a manual transmission and no brakes. As long as the engine is running and the clutch is out, the car will get to the top of the hill. But if you put in the clutch, you'll lose momentum and eventually start rolling backward. You need to maintain forward momentum to keep this from happening. If you're trying to help someone recover from an addiction, it's important to maintain a relationship with them and regularly ask how things are going with their recovery efforts. When things are at their best, plan for ways to recognize a loss of momentum and how to respond when such occurs.

A **lapse** is an isolated setback. A recovering alcoholic having one beer at a picnic, a recovering compulsive gambler buying one lottery ticket, a recovering drug addict taking a handful of caffeine pills when he feels tired. This single event is a serious issue, even though the person having the lapse may regard it as minor. Some refer to these setbacks as "slips." I look at "slip" as an acronym for Serious Lapse In Program. If you're helping someone that has just had a lapse, it's time to encourage a serious recommitment to the recovery plan that allowed them to achieve initial recovery. Encourage them to look at this as a speed bump, rather than a cliff—return to the path as quickly as possible with renewed vigor. Showing appreciation for their honesty is also valuable, as it will encourage them to come to you again if they struggle in the future. Accountability is vital in preventing a lapse from going beyond a single occurrence.

A **relapse** is a full return to a pattern of addiction. It is what the Bible describes as "a dog returning to its vomit" (2 Peter 2:22). At this point the recovery process the addict had committed to has been abandoned. Chances are, when this occurs, any help you've been offering the person will be rejected. If you are able to communicate with them, this is not the time for harsh judgment but for compassion, honest appraisal, and encouragement. If your offer of help is rejected, voice your being open to help in the future if they decide to seek recovery again. I've found there is no need to badger someone back into recovery— the addiction will do that for you. They will again suffer the consequences of their addiction, and when they do, it's important they know you will be a safe, supportive resource they can go to.

Here's an easy tool I developed to help organize a person's relapse prevention plan:

RELAPSE PREVENTION PLAN
List the top three risk areas you know you'll have to face.
    List two effective responses to each of those risk areas.
    List three emotional responses you need to be on guard for.
    List the top three support/accountability sources you will rely on.
    List three specific structure needs you have (going to 12-step meeting, attending worship services, Bible reading, etc.)
    List three successes you've had thus far in recovery that you intend to build on.

After completing this plan, it's helpful to arrange a time to review how well it was followed in six months or so. There are those that will complete a new plan every year to ensure they stay on the right track.

I'VE BEEN ASKED HOW TO COERCE SOMEONE THAT HAS returned to their addiction to repent; the Bible outlines the process in Galatians 6:1 "Brethren, if a man is overtaken in any trespass, you who are spiritual should restore such a one in a spirit of gentleness, considering yourself lest you also be tempted." Three considerations are given here: 1. You who are spiritual: Make sure you are on sound spiritual footing before you venture to help someone else. You won't be effective in saving someone from drowning if you're not a very good swimmer yourself. 2. Restore gently: Don't be timid about calling a sin a sin but consider how you can provide positive encouragement rather than harsh criticism. 3. Lest you be tempted: Of course, if you are helping to restore an alcoholic that has relapsed, having a few beers with them to talk it over isn't the answer. Also, you may not be tempted to engage in the person's addiction, but rather be tempted to condemn or to gossip. Consider how your disappointment with the person's behavior has impacted your own behavior. If you can't be objective and loving because you feel betrayed, maybe someone else would be better at trying to restore the person having a relapse.

WHAT WORKS AND WHAT DOESN'T

Rather than specific DOs and DON'Ts, I'd like to give a few observations in this section on what I've seen work in dealing with addicts seeking recovery and what I've seen cause more harm than good.

IT WORKS to be an example of personal change. By embarking on your own journey of recovery from the sin issues that have plagued you and being open to discussing your own recovery with others, you can become a fellow warrior with those battling a similar foe.

IT WORKS to foster an atmosphere of open communication about difficult and challenging subjects. Secrets and private temptations grow in the dark and shrink in the light of day, so be open to discussing such with acceptance and love.

IT WORKS to be informed about local resources and recovery groups. Being able to give a firsthand description of your experience attending a Celebrate Recovery group or your conversation with a Christian counselor is much more compelling than simply suggesting an online search.

IT WORKS to be patient and consistent. Enjoy the journey of recovery rather than seeking to "get this behind us." Sustaining an accountability relationship will help you and the other person. I'd recommend establishing a set time to check in so both you and the other person know to devote a time for communication.

IT WORKS to listen, rather than preach. Giving others the time and opportunity to vent can be the most productive thing you do. The best thing Job's friends did after he suffered unbelievable loss was to sit with him silently. The trouble started when they began talking. You were given two ears and one tongue for a reason—we should be "swift to hear, slow to speak" (James 1:19).

IT DOESN'T WORK to assume all is well without asking. Those that have never been caught up in a particular addiction may find it easy to think "they're free of it now; it'll never be a problem again." Asking how a person is doing in a spirit of encouragement can help sustain a connection and leave the door open if/when the person does have struggles.

IT DOESN'T WORK to look at recovering addicts as somehow different from others. It's easy to look at recovery programs as being for "those people." In Celebrate Recovery there are T-shirts that read "I'm One of Those People." On some level, we all are.

IT DOESN'T WORK to ignore your own limitations. Don't try to help someone up a mountain you've never climbed. Instead, find an experienced guide you can go to for input or that can help those beyond your capacity.

IT DOESN'T WORK to minimize how serious an addiction has become. If you're too close to a problem or honestly don't know how to determine how serious an addiction may have become, getting an objective evaluation is a good idea. It's also a useful strategy, when someone is denying the significance of an addiction, to suggest letting an objective addiction professional decide.

IT DOESN'T WORK to assume relapse will never happen, or to have the attitude that everyone relapses. I've heard people say, "Relapse is a part of recovery." Nope. Relapse is a part of addiction, and needs to be taken seriously. I expect all addicts to eventually have struggles, but to expect failure is to invite failure.

Suggestions

Here are three easy things you can do to aid your ability to help others with addictions:

1. Check out local Celebrate Recovery groups, either to inform yourself on how they operate or to see if you can benefit personally from what they offer.

2. Ask around your personal congregation to see who has recovery experience and may be willing to talk with others struggling with addiction.

3. Pray for those that deal with addictions.

Chapter Three

CODEPENDENCY

The term "codependency" has been around for decades, but unlike substance use disorders or depression there is no clearly defined "disorder" labeled codependency. While many definitions of this issue exist, they seem to fall into two categories: describing the relationship a person has with someone struggling with addiction, or describing the set of behaviors a person has in their relationship with others. For the sake of discussion let me offer a simple definition that melds the two: codependency is the condition of focusing so much attention on another person's addiction or other behavior that it negatively impacts your own behavior. Just as an addict focuses more and more of their attention on a drug, a codependent focuses more and more of their attention on the addict.

This leads to a host of negative behaviors, such as trying to control the other person (through watching their every move, pouring out alcohol/drugs, checking their phone, etc.), covering up the consequences of their addiction (calling in sick for them, taking on an inordinate amount of their financial burdens, making excuses for them), and/or worrying yourself sick over their behavior. I heard one codependent describe complaining about her husband's drinking to a cashier that was ringing up the beer she was buying him. The joke I've heard is, if a codependent is drowning, the other person's life flashes before their eyes. Its living life as a reaction, rather than as an independent being.

I've seen many Christians get caught up in codependency. Addictions can occur in any household, and it's a rare person that can deal with such without some personal negative impact. Its natural and healthy to want to help a friend or family member that struggles with addiction, but when it starts to interfere significantly with your ability to live your own life and you find your happiness is wrapped up in the other person's behavior, it's time to seek some help for yourself. Also, if you've been impacted by addiction in your childhood or in a past relationship, the negative impact may linger and have an effect on current relationships.

It can be a challenge when someone in the Church comes to you and says, "I just don't know what to do—they keep drinking and doing drugs, and I can't make them stop! You've got to help me!" The biggest initial hurdle I've been faced with in situations like this is that the person isn't wanting me to help **them**, they want me to tell them how they can fix the other person. I have disappointed many codependents by shifting the conversation to how they're taking care of themselves, how they're getting their own emotional support, and how they're developing healthy boundaries.

DETACHMENT

Just as Alcoholics Anonymous exists to help alcoholics recover through mutual support, Al-anon exists to help friends and family members of people with alcoholism. There are similar programs for other addictions, such as Nar-anon and Gam-anon to provide mutual support to friends and family members of other addictions. While these programs are "spiritual," rather than "religious," they address God "as you understand him" in the same manner as A.A. One of the most significant principles in all these programs is the principle of detachment. In a document Al-anon makes available to anyone (**https://al-anon.org/pdf/S19.pdf**) detachment is described as learning not to suffer when an alcoholic drinks and messes up their life, letting go of the illusion you can control anyone's addiction and focusing on personal happiness. People that are good at this find their own sense of contentment and happiness no matter what others do. It doesn't mean they have no concern for others, quite the opposite. Loving someone doesn't mean suffering with them. It means you share your concerns in a noncontrolling manner, make it clear that you will not enmesh yourself in their addictive behavior and that you will seek help for yourself. In Paul's many letters, he describes his deep emotions for the many Christians and congregations he had encountered and shares his sorrow for what many of them were going through, but he also stated he had learned the secret of being content in all circumstances. Detachment can provide such contentment for those enmeshed in someone else's addiction.

SETTING APPROPRIATE BOUNDARIES IS INHERENT IN THE process of detachment. The analogy I use is: If I have a neighbor with a big dog that keeps digging in my yard and I build a fence, I don't expect the fence to change the dog. If the dog gets over the fence and digs in my yard again, it's because my fence isn't effective. When setting boundaries with others, it's important to know what you can control and what you can't. It doesn't help to tell an addict you're married to, "I'll never speak to you again if you don't stop using," because you'll probably keep speaking, very loudly, if they keep using. Better to say, "I'm not going to bail you out of jail anymore and I'm not going to give you any more cash." Setting boundaries can seem harsh and should not be an excuse to shun or punish others. The purpose is to stay protected from potentially damaging relationships. Doing so while also being open to others is a balancing act, but you can learn to take thoughtful risks with others and to stick to sensible limits.

So how can you help a person struggling with codependency? Letting them know about the principles of detachment and about the support groups mentioned above are two ways. As Celebrate Recovery deals with all hurts, habits, and hang-ups, that is another option, with the focus remaining on Christ rather than generic spirituality. In fact, only one out of three members of Celebrate Recovery attend due to an alcohol or drug problem. Codependency is one of the other issues many who attend struggle with. Just as accountability is important for those in recovery from addiction, accountability is also vital for those struggling with codependency. A word of warning, be careful not to become enmeshed in a codependent's world. You may have to set your own boundaries in your relationship with the person you're trying to help. For example, you may have to limit the number of calls you're willing to take or limit the hours at which you'll accept calls. You may have to say, "I think that's a decision you'll have to make" many times. Or you may have to continually express the importance of the codependent letting go of control.

To encourage a codependent to let go and let an addict suffer through the ups and downs of their addiction, I tell the story of a man looking out his kitchen window and seeing a caterpillar spin a cocoon. He's excited to think he'll see a butterfly emerge, so he waits patiently. Eventually, he sees a crack in the cocoon and watches the butterfly struggle to get out. After this goes on for a while, he decides to help the butterfly by making a careful slit in the cocoon with a utility knife, and sure enough, the butterfly exits the cocoon easily. The man notices, however, the butterfly's wings look disproportionately small and its body overly large. He hopes the butterfly will grow out of this, but it never does. He learns that the effort a butterfly goes through to free itself from the cocoon squeezes fluid from its body and helps its wings develop—if it doesn't struggle, it will never fly. A codependent mother will balk at the idea of allowing her "poor baby" to suffer through the consequences of his actions, but if there's no struggle, why would anyone want to change? We do those we love a disservice by taking away their ability to learn from their mistakes, even if those lessons include a degree of suffering. Suffering is often the pathway to peace.

CARE GIVING VS. CARE TAKING

I am a care giver. My wife is disabled and in a wheelchair; she requires me to give her care that she cannot give herself. Before we married, she received this care from professionals. After we married, she had me! I was intimidated, as I have no special training in home healthcare; but I've learned a lot in the years we've been together. It would be foolish and pretty codependent of me to think I know better than my wife what she needs. Care givers provide needed aid the other person requires and has requested, in service to the person they are caring for. A care **taker**, on the other hand, is someone that feels they have the authority over someone they perceive as in need. They know best what that person needs, and they can decide how best to meet that need. Many codependents are care takers: they want to be in charge of making sure the other person has what they think they need, and they don't want their authority questioned. If the person can and should provide for themselves, a care taker won't allow it, because they know best. I don't want my no-good son working some menial job, even though it may lead him to some semblance of independence. I'd rather have him sleep on my couch and me pay for his needs, even though I complain about it constantly. An illustration in my wife's situation may help clarify: She needs me to pull her back in her chair several times a day to keep her balanced and comfortable. As a care giver, I do so when she asks. A care taker would announce "You need to be pulled back" whether she asks or not, or say "I just pulled you back a few minutes ago" if they didn't think adjustment was necessary. I think you can see the difference.

AS A PERSON HELPING SOMEONE THAT HAS TAKEN ON A care taker role, it's important to refocus them on what the person they're trying to control really wants and needs. "How have they tried to do that themselves?" is a good question to ask. The sooner a care taker can relinquish control, the freer they will become.

DOs and DON'Ts

DO maintain a high degree of personal autonomy and contentment when dealing with others struggling with codependency. As mentioned earlier, be that solid object in a sea of turmoil.

DO stay focused on what the codependent is doing, rather than get into indictments of the their behavior.

DO expose yourself to support groups for codependents. This will give you a better understanding of what's available in your area.

DO examine your own boundaries. Are you effective in protecting yourself from toxic intrusions while maintaining an open stance with those in need?

DO pray for codependents struggling in relationships with addicts, and for yourself, as you endeavor to help them.

DON'T allow yourself to become enmeshed in the relationship drama of others. Remain calm and concerned while maintaining your focus on how you can help the codependent in need.

DON'T think you have to help alone! Seeking personal support is important. You may also need to seek guidance from professionals or more experienced sources when you find yourself beyond your capacity.

DON'T simply give up on trying to help in high-drama, dysfunctional situations. It can be very rewarding to be able to support others and God may be calling you, specifically, to help in this situation.

DON'T be afraid to call codependency what it is. When I've been bombarded with a litany of descriptions of how bad the addict is, I have usually simply asked, "Have you ever heard of Al-anon?" The complete change in demeanor I often see in the codependent tells me clearly they aren't looking at how to change themselves, but how to fix their family member/friend.

DON'T get discouraged! A popular quip in recovery circles is "Don't quit until the miracle happens." Even if you don't see any significant improvement today, the benefits you and the other person receive from talking through the problem and potential solutions can help the two of you build invaluable bonds with each other, as well as stronger relationships with God.

Suggestions

Here are three quick, easy things you can do to promote your ability to help codependents in need:

1. Go to an Al-anon, Celebrate Recovery, or other group in your area that provides mutual support to codependents.

2. Examine your own boundaries and work on being both open to others and secure from toxic enmeshment.

3. Investigate who in your congregation or circle of associates has been successful in addressing their own codependency; ask them if they'd be interested in talking with those in need.

Chapter Four

ANGER

The Bible has a wealth of things to say about anger. From the simple statement by Paul in Ephesians 4:26, "Be angry, and do not sin: do not let the sun go down on your wrath, nor give place to the devil," to Jesus telling us to "turn the other cheek," we are clearly expected to prevent the emotion of anger from leading us to go against God's will. Yet many of us have felt the heat of anger and found ourselves saying and doing things we regret. Also, we may have been raised in an environment in which anger was not dealt with properly and learned very irresponsible anger-response habits. I know of a teen in a group home that returned from a family visit with a black eye. When asked what happened, he simply stated, "I told a lie." When staff stated that telling a lie doesn't cause a black eye, the teen just shrugged and said, "It does at my house." This teen is likely to come up swinging when angry as this is what he'd witnessed in his home environment. The key to effective, nonsinful anger response is to separate the emotion from the reaction. As the verse above indicates, the sin is not in the emotion, but in the response. So how do we develop a healthy response to anger? And how do we help those that have fallen into unhealthy anger-response patterns?

I WOULD LIKE TO SHARE A PRESENTATION I GIVE ON THE different responses people can have to conflict. It's based on differentiating between respecting another person and sticking up for ourselves. In a moment of conflict, there are four different options of response:

> Passive—We might call this being a doormat, a pushover, or a wimp. I use the example of a henpecked husband whose wife says, "Leonard, take out the garbage!" He responds, "Yes, dear!", but the whole way out to the trash can he grumbles under his breath, "Why do I always have to take out the garbage? She's always making me take out the garbage." Leonard is being passive—he is respecting his wife's wishes but he's not sticking up for himself. Why are people passive? Because they don't want to upset the other person. They are more concerned about how their behavior will impact the other person than they are about meeting their own emotional needs. Passive people can often have the highest level of underlying anger, but they keep it buried. The problem with this is you don't bury anger dead; you bury it alive. It will dig itself out in some manner; whether it takes the form of high blood pressure, ulcers, or an eventual unbalanced blowup, the anger won't stay buried forever.
>
> Aggressive—This is being a bully, being hostile. In the example of Leonard being asked to take out the garbage, the aggressive response would be, "What's the matter, are your legs broken? Get it yourself you Bleep Bleep Bleep." Here, Leonard is being aggressive—he's sticking

up for himself, but he is not respecting his wife. Many people with anger problems act aggressively. Why? Because it works! Bullies get the lunch money. The focus of an aggressive person is on winning. They want to control, belittle, or attack the person that makes them mad. Many an aggressive person has justified their hurtful actions by pointing out how the other person triggered their anger. They are looking at the other person's behavior, not at their own.

Passive-Aggressive—This is being sarcastic or duplicitous. In the example of Leonard being asked to take out the garbage, a passive-aggressive response would be saying things like, "Well, of course! Whatever the queen wants!" or taking out one milk carton and later saying, "Oh, did you mean take out all the garbage?" This isn't as hostile as straight aggression and isn't as submissive as straight passivity, but it is designed to get a reaction from the other person. It seems sitcoms on television often celebrate sarcasm, but this is not the way to turn the other cheek. A person that acts passive-aggressively is looking for a way to get a subtle jab in without coming off openly hostile. Again, the focus is on the other person and how you can evoke a reaction.

Assertive—Of course, the goal when angry or in any confrontation is to respond assertively. Assertiveness involves focusing on one's own behavior and determining whether the response is right and appropriate, not whether or not you'll get the response you're hoping for from the other person. In the example with Leonard there are three different ways he can be assertive: 1. Take out the garbage and don't grumble. If you can feel good about submitting to another person, as in turning the other cheek, everybody wins. Of course, always being a doormat isn't likely to make you feel good all the time, and getting a reputation as someone that can be pushed around may lead to negative consequences. 2. Say, "It seems like I take out the garbage most of the time. How about if I take it out this time, you take it out next time, and we compromise?" Many situations that anger us have an available, mutually beneficial solution if we're willing to look for it. 3. Leonard may not be able to take out the garbage, either because of an established agreement that it isn't his job or some pressing matter of greater importance. Leonard will need to then say, "I'm sorry, but I'm not going to be taking out the garbage." His wife may come back telling him what a lazy bum he is, but Leonard just politely sticks to his guns and calmly says he isn't going to comply. Understand, being assertive is its own reward. It has the best chance of soliciting an assertive response, but even if it doesn't, you can feel good knowing your behavior was appropriate. In any situation where anger is triggered, the faster a person can begin examining their options for an assertive response the less power the anger will have.

They tell the story of a seasoned, full-bodied monk sitting under a tree when an angry person comes by and starts calling him a fat, ugly, good-for-nothing lazy slob, continuing the rant for an extended period while the monk sits and smiles. When the angry person finally runs out of breath, the monk asks him, "If someone tries to give you a present, and you don't accept it, who does the present belong to?"

The person replies, "I guess the person trying to give the present." The monk replies, "Then take your present, and be on your way." Just because someone is trying to get us to respond in an angry manner doesn't mean we're obligated to do so. One of my favorite verses is Proverbs 25:21 & 22—"If your enemy is hungry, give him bread to eat; And if he is thirsty, give him water to drink; For *so* you will heap coals of fire on his head, and the Lord will reward you." The purpose, of course, is not to tick the other person off but to behave in a way consistent with God's will.

Another great saying is "What would be the right thing to do if I didn't feel this way?" Your feelings often give you terrible advice on the appropriate response to someone else. If you weren't angry, what would be the most Godly response in this situation? If you only had $50 worth of anger to last you the rest of your life, would it be worth investing some of that in this issue? If we become stingier with our anger, we'll discover that many battles don't need to be fought. Of course, as in the example of Jesus turning over tables in the temple, there are some issues that demand giving action to our anger, but we can seek to do so in an assertive, gentle, Godly manner.

You can also help a person with an anger problem by helping them find a diverting activity that can help them channel their anger. At the last program I worked for they took the guys to the gym every weekday. Many of them said it helped them immensely and was one of the biggest assets to the program. I had a college professor that talked about the misguided notion of "mind-body dualism." This is the idea that you have a mind and a body and the two are somehow separate. No! They are completely intertwined. I would add our spirit to this formula. There is nothing that impacts our physical health that doesn't also impact our mental health and spiritual well-being. If we improve our physical activity, it will aid in any emotional issue we struggle with and we will have a spiritual benefit as well.

One more skill in dealing with anger is known as "reframing." This is the idea that the ugliest picture in the world would look better in a nice frame. If you look at a negative situation as an opportunity rather than just a frustration, you may be able to let go of your anger. The best example I've heard has to do with the development of Post-it notes. The scientist that developed the adhesive for the well-known product did so by accident—he was trying to develop a super strong adhesive and instead developed one that was weak and reusable. If he had focused on being angry about not making the discovery he was hoping for, he might have missed out on developing a multi-million-dollar product.

Becoming personally proficient in these skills will give us the capacity to help others through their anger issues and will help us from suffering the consequences of our own anger. As with other issues, being an example of how to handle anger in a Godly manner may be the best help you can provide.

RESENTMENT
The word resentment comes from Latin, meaning to re-feel, or feel again and again. We're not just mad, we're repeatedly mad. We hold on to a hurt or injustice we've experienced and refuse to let it go. Why do we hold resentments? Because we don't want to let the person that hurt us get away with it. The problem is, our resentment is hurting us, not the other person. Carrie Fisher famously quoted St. Augustine,

"Resentment is like drinking poison hoping the other person will die." Honestly, how much sense does it make to stay up at night being mad at someone that's getting a good night's sleep? Who's going to be tired in the morning?

Some will respond, "But you don't understand how bad they hurt me." I would never want to belittle the pain and trauma people have experienced at the hands of others. I'll look at trauma in a later chapter. It's just that resentment doesn't help the healing process and can do additional damage to the one that resents.

So how do we help those caught up in resentment?

THE MAIN TASK IN LETTING GO OF RESENTMENTS, OF course, is forgiveness. There are three things to consider in forgiving others, any of which can be a hang-up for people stuck in resentments. 1) Hurt people hurt other people. The person that hurt us was likely hurt themselves. Do you want to become a hurt person that hurts others? If not, then you need to give your hurt to God. We will never come close to being hurt at the same level Jesus was while going to the cross for our sins, yet one of the last things he said was, "Forgive them, they know not what they do" (Luke 23:34). 2) Forgiveness can take place long before the pain goes away. In fact, forgiving can help the healing process. Even if the pain persists we can intellectually resolve to not actively hold on to the resentment. 3) We will be free to help others more effectively when we can finally forgive those that hurt us. The Bible has several verses that speak to us about being forgiven by the same measure we forgive others; you can ask a person struggling with resentment how that measuring stick is working for them.

DOs and DON'Ts

DO encourage the person caught up in anger to seek a centering activity when angry, like counting to ten, breathing in God's peace, or recalling a scripture. Being mindful of my actions is the best way to move from anger to resolution.

DO encourage the person battling with resentment to write a letter to the person they resent and then shred it, rather than sending it. You can get the emotions out and let them go in a tangible expression.

DO encourage the person battling resentment to pray for the source of their resentment. Pray for their well-being, not for God's wrath on the person. You won't be able to keep a resentment against a person you sincerely want God to bless.

DO track successes in letting go of anger rather than just focusing on times of angry outbursts.

DO seek the best assertive response in any conflict.

DON'T let yourself get caught up in being angry at those that have harmed those you care about. Model forgiveness whenever possible.

DON'T simply ask a person to "get over it." Their pain is real. Focus instead on the next step toward healing, even though the pain may persist.

DON'T let your own unresolved anger or resentment cloud your ability to help others with the same issue.

DON'T drop the ball if you've agreed to be an accountability partner. Stick to the communication arrangement you've made.

DON'T forget to pray for those that are caught up in anger or resentment.

Suggestions

Here are three easy things you can do to aid your ability to help others with anger issues:

1. Have in mind several examples of the benefits of forgiveness, whether from the Bible (e.g., Esau forgiving Jacob) or from your personal experience.

2. Prepare for follow through with accountability agreements.

3. Practice assertiveness in all conflicts you face. You'll then be more skilled in finding the best assertive response when helping others.

Chapter Five

MARITAL/FAMILY ISSUES

The concept of "family" has changed dramatically since I was a child. Though there were certainly divorces in the '50s and '60s, it was more or less expected that young men and women would grow to adulthood, get and stay married, have children, and hopefully live to see many grandchildren. If this didn't happen, something was thought to have gone wrong. The world of the Bible certainly revolved around the nuclear family. There are many verses, proverbs, and parables devoted to the proper ways to behave in our roles as husbands, wives, sons, and daughters. Over the years, the idea of two people getting married, then having children and remaining married for the rest of their lives has become to many an outdated concept. Polls indicate the majority of young people do not see the necessity of marriage or children; the concept of being male or female as assigned at birth has even been open to debate. As a result, it's no wonder many in the Church experience marital difficulties and parenting conflicts, and many have suffered divorce. There are many good, Christ-centered books on marriage and parenting, so I won't try to recreate what's already been published, but I believe there are important considerations when trying to help families through these struggles.

THE PRINCIPLES OF FAMILY DYNAMICS

The concept of family dynamics has been a part of many therapy models for decades, all of which are based on the idea that our first experience with a system is the family we grow up in. We learn who has authority, what the rules are, the opportunities available to us, and the ways in which we can receive love and/or approval. I'm sure, just by reading these words you can think of families (perhaps even your own) where this system has gone horribly wrong. The parents that were supposed to be loving leaders and guides have either become tyrants or unconcerned with their children. Husbands have rejected the idea of loving their wives "as Christ loved the Church" (Ephesians 5:25) and instead treat them as slaves or convenient punching bags (literally or metaphorically). Wives have rejected the idea of submitting to their husbands and have instead demanded to be the primary authority, treating their husbands with disdain. Children have rejected the idea of obeying their parents and instead demand that their whims be met or else they will make the lives of their parents miserable. I'd love to tell you these extremes never happen in the Church but I'm sure you've experienced some degree of these types of problems or know someone who has.

There's no one cause for family discord, but I believe selfishness is as common a factor as you'll find in most situations. Society promotes self-love and striving to get what you want. This will not work in a Godly family where the needs of others must be considered. Philippians 2:3-4 states, "Let nothing be done through selfish ambition or conceit, but in lowliness of mind let each esteem others better than himself. Let each of you look out not only for his own interests, but also for the interests of others."

For issues between husbands and wives, the best model I've seen comes from the book *His Needs/Her Needs— Building an Affair-Proof Marriage* by Willard F. Harley, Jr. (2011). The philosophy of this model is that if you want to be happy in your marriage, create an environment where your spouse is the happiest, the most content they can be. We all have needs, from recognition to intimacy to security. You can't expect your spouse to be intimate if they're living in fear of bankruptcy or have been belittled every day. The key is to truly discover your spouse's needs and work to promote an environment where those needs can be met.

If you think this sounds like a contradiction to the description of detachment, look closer—the goal is not to react to your spouse's demands or take responsibility for their lives but to consider how you can be an encouraging, nurturing partner in their efforts to be who God designed them to be. If you do so, you'll find your spouse to be highly motivated in helping you meet your needs.

When helping someone through their marital struggles, discussing this concept can be very helpful, especially when followed by an examination of how marital conflict arose. Quite often the root is one or both partners not having a particular need met. I've even been told, by someone in marital strife, that they had no intention of giving their spouse what they needed until their own needs were met. Marriage is not a 50/50 proposition—it is 100/100. I am 100 percent responsible for my role as a husband regardless of what my wife does. She is likewise 100 percent responsible for her role, no matter how much of a jerk I'm being. If that sounds unfair, you're getting the right idea. "For better or worse" isn't meant to be fair. It can be difficult to help someone focus on their own behavior choices, especially if their spouse is behaving inappropriately, but that's the focus that you need to promote. Commiserating about what a jerk someone's spouse is being won't improve that person's marriage; looking at personal behavior and what changes can be made might.

Frequent questions that arise include, "What do I do if my husband or wife is being abusive, won't go to work, constantly screams at the kids, or does something else that is totally intolerable?" No one is expected to stay in an unsafe or unsustainable system, but no system starts out this dysfunctional. By examining the progression into the dysfunctional state, looking at how the system veered off into the way it works now, determining how committed both parties are to make it work and how much support will be needed to heal what needs to be healed, you can help others no matter how bad things have gotten.

The concept of the Love Bank is part of the His Needs/Her Needs book. Briefly stated, when you start a new relationship you open an "account" with that person. When they make you happy, a deposit is made. When they do something that results in unhappiness, a withdrawal is made. When the balance gets high enough, you become willing to make a commitment to the relationship and eventually may be ready to marry. The problem is, the moment you move in together the deposits will likely start to drop off and the withdrawals may come more often. Eventually, some accounts become overdrawn. If you're in a committed relationship, what do you do? Some people reach a point where they aren't willing to leave the relationship, but they have no faith they will experience more happiness than unhappiness, so they wall themselves off from the conflict and go into a state of withdrawal from their spouse. This is often the point a person will be in when they seek help for their marriage.

I'm sorry to say it, but you can't get back to an intimate relationship, where you experience more happiness than unhappiness, without slogging through the many withdrawals that have been made. The goal is to become teammates again. You don't want a situation where one spouse is on one side of a problem and the other spouse is on the other side, both clinging bitterly to winning rather than coming to a resolution. You want to help them to come up beside their mate, and ask, "What can we do to resolve this problem together?" Hopefully they're still interested in being teammates.

If someone (or their mate) has little or no interest in stopping the source of the withdrawals or resolving conflicts, the relationship may be doomed. At this point I would recommend determining whether both parties are in, out, or waiting. "In" means I am committed to the relationship and I want to make it work. I'm willing to put in hard work and I understand there may be pain in the process, pain that can eventually lead to harmony. "Out" means I am done; I refuse to consider continuing in the relationship and all I want to do is clean up loose ends. At this point, admonition from others in the church or concerns about how separation will impact the children mean little. I have no willingness to give any effort to salvaging the marriage. "Waiting" means I can't make a firm decision about being in or out. Some days I feel there might be a chance, some days I feel it's hopeless. I'm willing, at times, to try to reconcile but I easily give up my resolve when any troubles surface. The relative security of going back to withdrawal is inviting.

If the people you're working with can't commit to being in or out, encourage them to make a decision to wait, let's say, six months, while they get themselves on sound footing. Bouncing between in and out is unnerving; if a person can't commit to one or the other, committing to a wait period is likely the best option. There's a lot of work to be done during this period of waiting, work that can be better accomplished if the person isn't burdened with a decision of whether or not to end the relationship. Once the time period is over, they will hopefully be in a better place to make a decision about in or out; if not, they can always opt to wait for another few months. If someone you're working with opts for a wait period, it's important to work through how they will use that time to work on themselves, develop healthy coping skills and seek the support they need. There are those I've worked with that have developed their strongest relationship with God during a time of waiting. In both situations where marital reconciliation was possible and where it was not, I've seen people maintain their heightened sense of spiritual commitment because of the work they did during these wait periods.

YOU MAY VERY WELL ENCOUNTER A PERSON THAT NEEDS help after their spouse has already left. The song "Who Will Be Jesus" by Bruce Carroll begins with the plight of a man coming to church, sitting alone for the first time after his wife left him, feeling the eyes on him and his heart breaking. Being Jesus to this man means going to him with comfort and love, rather than judgment, and discussing how he can remain connected to God through his pain. There are programs that can help those suffering divorce. DivorceCare identifies themselves as "the #1 Divorce Recovery Program in the World." It involves a thirteen-week, video-based series where those struggling with divorce or separation can find healing and mutual support.

GENERATIONAL DYSFUNCTION

We tend to think the families we grow up in are pretty normal. I happened to grow up in a family where my dad drank heavily and my mother reacted in a codependent manner. It wasn't until I was in junior high that I discovered this wasn't "normal," and it wasn't until much later that I realized how many of my own behavior patterns developed while growing up in this system. A substantial portion of the way I learned to interact originated through what I experienced in childhood. We don't know what we don't know, so it's important to humbly examine how we function in our immediate family relationships if we want to eventually be the husbands and wives God calls us to be. Someone coming to you for help with a marital issue may not realize why their spouse isn't acting the way they expected. A speaker I once heard, describing her own codependent expectations, shared this: "I always thought of love as a heart-shaped, red box of chocolates. My husband would bring me a square box of caramels. I'd say, 'Why don't you love me?' And he'd say, 'I did.'" We need to recognize the expressions of love given by those close to us even when they don't appear as we expect them.

I SAW A GREAT TRAINING VIDEO WHERE A CHRISTIAN marital therapist described his first marriage counseling case, and the problem the couple had with underwear. On their first night together after their honeymoon the husband had left his dirty underwear in the middle of the floor. The next night the underwear was still there, and neither partner had said anything about it. The husband deposited his dirty underwear on top of the other pair, and at the end of the week there was a pile of seven pairs of dirty underwear. Rather than talk to each other about it, the husband just bought a bunch of new underwear and at the end of the month they had come in for marriage counseling due to a pile of thirty pairs of dirty underwear.

The counselor handled this easily. He asked them what the problem was. The husband answered, "My mother didn't expect my dad to do all the work, she kept the house clean and did all the laundry." The wife answered, "My dad didn't expect my mom to wait on him hand and foot, he contributed to the household chores." The counselor asked the husband if he would be willing to put his underwear in a hamper near his pile if his wife washed them for him; the husband thought this was okay. The counselor then asked the wife if she would wash them if the husband put them in the hamper; she agreed that was all she expected him to do. Problem solved! So why couldn't this couple solve the problem themselves? Because they came into the marriage expecting things to be a certain way, and when it wasn't they looked for a way to get their expectations met rather than a way to meet the other's needs.

There are many marriage enrichment seminars, books, retreats, videos, groups, and conferences but none of them are likely to work if a couple can't come to an agreement on what to expect. Premarital counseling is optimally designed to resolve this problem, but many in the Church never had this type of counseling, never took it seriously or never did the work to come to an agreement. When I work with a couple in marital therapy, I start by asking them three questions: What do you need from your spouse? What does your spouse need from you? and What will you absolutely not tolerate? It's important that both parties have their answers prepared before they share them with each other. I am amazed at how different the answers often are. Many people have no true idea what their spouse needs or even what they expect from their spouse. Some haven't even considered what they really need in their marriage. Also, many people say they won't tolerate a behavior but continue to tolerate it for many years. You may say, "I can't take it anymore," but the truth is you've probably gotten pretty good at taking it. You just don't know how to take it without being miserable. If that's the case, the previous description of detachment will be your key to peace.

EFFECTIVE PARENTING
If marriage is met with confusion and doubt in today's society, parenting seems to have met with even more confusion. When the White House indicates that children don't belong to parents but to all of society, Christian parents trying to raise their children according to biblical principles often feel under attack. You're probably not going to get very far by telling someone else how to parent their children, but there are some basic principles that can be helpful when trying to aid someone experiencing parenting difficulties.

I've found that the two extremes of "rule with an iron hand" and "let them get away with anything" produce similar consequences. Parents that run their home like a military camp, answer each question with "because I said so," and inflict harsh punishment for every minor wrong generally get children that don't know the reason for the rules they are under, never learn how to discern limits for themselves because the limits are made for them, and usually seek opportunities to go against the rules when they believe they won't get caught. Parents that are so concerned with their children's self-esteem that they never set a limit and never learn to say no generally get children that don't know how to set limits for themselves and seek opportunities to go against the rules because they don't expect to experience any consequences at home for any of their behaviors.

The best, simplest parenting advice I ever heard came from an elder's wife: "Say yes as often as possible; when you say no, mean it." I think it's not only important to set rules in a Christian home, with well-understood consequences, but it is also important for children to understand the values that are behind those rules. In families with teenagers, I've recommended the teens be involved in drafting a list of family values, family expectations, and consequences. Of course, if your children are involved in drafting a list of values, you'll be expected to live by the same values. This doesn't mean parents don't have more freedoms and opportunities than children; parents carry far more responsibility so they should have more freedoms. It means that parents agree to adhere to family values.

I think it's also important that good behavior gets rewarded, rather than simply punishing bad behavior. My daughter has operated under a point system with my grandson for many years. He knows that doing his chores and obeying requests results in points, disobedience or failure to meet expectations results in lost points. Points can be used to get things he wants, so it helps him learn the value of money as well. She doesn't need to badger him, spank him, or ground him, all she has to do is say, "Do I need to take away a point?" and she immediately has an obedient child. This type of system takes a while to develop, but it can work well for many families.

The key is to avoid power struggles. If you have a written list of expectations, rewards, and consequences, the child is no longer fighting with you, they're fighting with a piece of paper. Children will plead and whine, but the paper remains the same. My previous statement about being the solid object in a river of turmoil comes to play in parenting. The best parenting is monotonous, time consuming, and sometimes draining, but will ultimately be rewarding. All children have things they want and virtually all will be willing to negotiate with assertive, values-driven parents, especially if they have a voice in the values clarification process. I heard a great analogy about avoiding power struggles: Admiral Blowhard was at the helm of a ship in completely blanketing fog when a blip appeared on the radar indicating they were on a collision course with another party up ahead. He quickly radioed the other party and announced they would need to move to a different course. The response came, "I'm sorry but we won't be able to do that. You're going to need to change your course." Admiral Blowhard shot back, "I'm not going to change my course! I'm Admiral Blowhard! You need to change your course!" The reply came, "This is a lighthouse. Your call." If you encourage a person experiencing parenting issues to stand firm, be respectful and state the foundations for the principles they are living by in their family, most power struggles can be avoided.

WHEN HELPING SOMEONE WITH PARENTING ISSUES, BE

"quick to hear, slow to speak" (James 1:19). Most parents I've worked with know the right thing to do and can agree to the principles I've indicated above; they're just frustrated at how difficult it can be in practice. Often what they need most is a chance to vent and validation that their values are still worth upholding.

Often two parents have very different values, which results in conflict with the children. The first task is to get the parents on the same page. In step-parenting situations this can be especially difficult. The principles remain the same—list values, expectations, consequences, and rewards for **your** house. The quicker you can encourage a struggling parent to focus on their own behavior the sooner you'll be able to help them through the conflicts they face.

WHAT IF MY SPOUSE OR KIDS AREN'T BELIEVERS?

This is a fairly common issue I've seen parents or married people seek help with. If you've been raised in a Christian household, you may be at a loss about how to aid someone that is a Christian but has family members that aren't. I personally was raised Catholic but had serious problems with Catholic doctrine, also seeing a great deal of hypocrisy. As mentioned earlier, I began recovery from my drug addiction at age seventeen and quickly adopted a God-as-you-understand-Him form of spirituality, finding no value in "organized" religion. This changed when my daughter was born—I didn't want her to learn about God through a 12-step program. I was invited to a Bible study by a friend at this time, and I attended with the intention of taking it right to the preacher leading the study. When he asked for questions at the end of the study I piped up, "Yeah, I have a question: Is Gandhi going to hell?" His answer was perfect. He said, "I don't make that determination, God does. I know I'm going to heaven. I'll find out if he's there when I get there." That is exactly what I needed to hear at that time, and that preacher baptized me a short time later. I was skeptical of religion, as many of our children and some of our spouses may be. I needed to know if all the talk about God was real; I didn't need to hear a lot of church talk or moralizing. Thankfully, there are many sources to answer spiritual questions objectively, and I would recommend every Christian acquaint themselves with a few of them.

The book *More Than a Carpenter* by Josh McDowell (1987) had a profound impact on me. In it, McDowell lays out a logical, objective analysis of Jesus's life, claims, death, and resurrection from a thoughtful, critical point of view. He also shares the famous quote from C.S. Lewis in *Mere Christianity*:

> "I am trying here to prevent anyone saying the really foolish thing that people often say about Him: I'm ready to accept Jesus as a great moral teacher, but I don't accept his claim to be God. That is the one thing we must not say. A man who was merely a man and said the sort of things Jesus said would not be a great moral teacher. He would either be a lunatic—on the level with the man who says he is a poached egg—or else he would be the Devil of Hell. You must make your choice. Either this man was, and is, the Son of God, or else a madman or something worse. You can shut him up for a fool, you can spit at him and kill him as a demon, or you can fall at his feet and call him Lord and God,

but let us not come with any patronizing nonsense about his being a great human teacher. He has not left that open to us. He did not intend to."

Other valuable books that accomplish the same task include Lee Strobel's *The Case For Christ* (2016) and *Cold Case Christianity* by J. Warner Wallace (2013).

God has many children, but no grandchildren. We must each come to Him on our own. We can make our children go to church, just as we make them go to school, but there's no way to force what they believe. The timetable for their coming to their own decision about Christ is in their hands. Especially in the teen years, pushing will likely meet with resistance. Likewise, if you are married to a nonbelieving spouse or you become a Christian after you marry, you can be a great example, but you can't force your mate into faith. As a person wanting to help someone with a nonbelieving family member, you can offer one of the above noted resources or perhaps share your own faith story.

DOs and DON'Ts

DO allow the person you're trying to help to vent what they're feeling before offering any advice.

DO find out how committed both parties are to working through marital conflicts.

DO explore family values in matters of parenting issues.

DO investigate Christian marital and family therapy options in your area or congregation.

DO show compassion to families embroiled in divorce or separation.

DON'T get triangulated in a couple's conflict.

DON'T moralize. Confront the sin but love the sinner.

DON'T blame parents or children in matters of parenting discord. Focus instead on the value system in the home and how to uphold it.

DON'T think you have no help to offer if you have no children, your children are out of the home, or you've experienced marital/parenting problems yourself. We can all be a listening ear and the voice of stability regardless of our experience.

DON'T get over your head. If there are serious issues beyond your experience or training, don't be afraid to seek help.

Suggestions

Here are three easy things you can do to aid your ability to help others with marital or parenting issues:

1. Discuss with staff in your congregation how they deal with marital problems, what they can and can't provide in the way of marital or family counseling, and who they refer to when a need arises.

2. Investigate success stories in your congregation from families that have made it through marital or parenting struggles.

3. Read one of the books listed above that objectively present the case for Christianity.

Chapter Six

TRAUMA

There are serious crises we are all vulnerable to, from assaults to accidents to untimely deaths. These can produce trauma, simply defined as our coping capacity being overwhelmed. There are two categories of trauma: Big-T trauma and little-t trauma. Big-T trauma includes events that overwhelm us even if they only happen once, such as a rape, a catastrophic car accident, or a murder. We can experience years of difficulty trying to resolve the impact of an event that lasts only a few minutes. Little-t trauma involves situations where we have repeated incidents that challenge our coping ability, such as being told we're an idiot every day or working in a highly dangerous job for years. If such a situation occurred just once we'd be able to handle it, but over time, our abilities become overwhelmed, and the trauma begins having its impact.

In any traumatic experience, our brains go into a response I liken to "going off-line." If someone points a gun at you, you don't want to stop and think through what you should do, you want your brain to just react automatically by causing you to duck. This automatic response can save your life. The problem is some people get stuck in this trauma response; every time they recall the event(s) their brain goes off-line. It's like they are experiencing the trauma all over again. This is the basic way Post Traumatic Stress Disorder (PTSD) works.

It's probably easier to list what doesn't work in dealing with trauma. Telling people to "get over it," ignoring the impact of trauma, exaggerating the trauma by making it sound impossible to deal with, and lumping everything into the category of spiritual warfare are just a few of the ways I've seen people respond to those suffering from trauma; none of those ways is likely to help.

I do believe we can aid people that have experienced serious trauma, but let me give a clear warning—serious trauma, especially PTSD, is likely to require professional help.

HOW TO HEAL

I experienced sexual abuse at a very young age and didn't fully comprehend the impact this had on me until decades later. The first step in healing is to acknowledge the damage that was done. I had to make peace with the little boy inside me that had been abused, and this process took a while. I had a terrific counselor that compared the healing process to her experience having to clean up after a drainpipe in her basement backed up. She explained that her first efforts to clean were miserable; she could only stay in the basement for a short time, and it didn't seem the mess was getting any better. But she knew she had to complete the job, so she kept at it every day until it finally started to look a little better. Eventually she could stay down there for longer periods, until she got to the drain that caused the problem and fixed it so it wouldn't back up in the future.

What an excellent description of how healing works! We acknowledge our trauma, dig right in to heal the pain we experienced, and keep at it until we're through. And "through" is the correct word. We don't get over trauma, we get through it. There are support groups for a variety of issues to help in this process, and trauma is one of the issues Celebrate Recovery can help with.

ONE OF THE MOST POPULAR THERAPY OPTIONS IN DEALing with trauma is Eye Movement Desensitization Reprocessing. It involves moving your eyes from side to side while processing the trauma with a trained therapist. I'll be honest, when I first heard about the technique I was beyond skeptical. After seeing EMDR speed up the healing process for dozens of people, I have come to have confidence in its effectiveness. This is specialized therapy, so it may take a while to locate a therapist trained in the technique, and even longer to locate a Christ-centered therapist so trained, but for those deeply stuck in trauma the search may be worth it.

ONCE YOU DO EXPERIENCE HEALING FROM YOUR OWN trauma, you will be uniquely qualified to aid others. Another valuable quip you'll hear in Celebrate Recovery is "God never wastes a hurt." Whatever we've made it through can be used to aid someone else. Though we may not have experienced a traumatic event exactly like the person we're trying to help, sharing how we experienced healing from our own trauma may be very inspirational.

VICTIMS VS. VICTORS

It is so sad to see people that have experienced abuse or other trauma in their past continue to be hurt by it. The worst example I ever heard was during a training given by a longtime trauma therapist. He described a patient he had that had been severely physically and sexually abused for years by her stepfather. When her mother and the stepfather had another child, she threw herself into caring for the baby. The stepfather, seeing this, murdered the baby right in front of her and told her it was her fault. The traumatized woman understandably asked, "Why would I ever trust anyone ever again?" I can only hope this woman received the healing she needed. Compare this to the young man suffering unimaginable abuse in the book *A Child Called It* (1985). I was blessed to have heard the author speak at a conference long ago, and he described devoting his life to honoring human service workers in gratitude for them rescuing him from an abusive mother that wouldn't even call him by his name. Both these two experienced far more trauma than most of us are ever likely to experience. Yet one chose to openly share his experience rather than to remain trapped in the trauma for endless years. I believe this is the best form of healing, proclaiming our victory over the pain we've experienced rather than prolonging the pain by keeping it hidden. The pain of trauma grows in the dark and shrinks in the light of day. If you're helping someone through their trauma, encourage them to share as openly as possible in a safe environment and take the power away from the trauma, putting the power back in God's hands where it belongs.

I have to give a warning—I've seen people take this too far and try to elicit sympathy by wearing their traumatic experiences like a badge of honor. It's important, as helpers, not to give just sympathy but empathy. Sympathy says, "Oh, you poor little thing," expressing how damaged we regard the person to be. Someone trying to elicit sympathy for their trauma will not be aided by this attitude and may in fact stay stuck longer if their self-pity is endorsed. Empathy says, "I can see that was very painful. Though I can never fully understand your pain, I have had very painful experiences in my life and have worked hard to get through them. Can I share with you what my journey has been like?" Hopefully, by helping someone resolve their trauma in an empathetic manner, your own healing will be enhanced, and you may gain a close friend in the process.

Here's a handout I have given to addiction groups on the subject of trauma:

TRAUMA MYTHS	
Trauma is	**Trauma is not**
A response to real or potential threat	An "over-reaction"
An automatic response	A sign of weakness
A disruption to life	An event we just "get over"
A potential threat to our recovery	A good excuse to use

RESPONSES TO TRAUMA	
Healthy	**Unhealty**
Talk about it	Stuff it inside
Share with others with similar experiences	Say "I'm over it"
Engage in behaviors that promote safety	Ignore safety needs

Find healthy ways to soothe emotions	Numb emotions
Develop a sense of structure	Live haphazardly
Prepare for triggering events	Live with the panic
Seek support promptly	Handle it "on my own"
Believe I'm a competent survivor	Stay a victim

DOs and DON'Ts

DO share your own healing from trauma experiences in appropriate settings.

DO seek resources available in your area for those experiencing the effects of trauma.

DO listen to those who just need to share about their trauma experiences.

DO provide empathy, rather than just sympathy.

DO ensure you've effectively worked through your own trauma experiences before endeavoring to help others.

DON'T try to blame the victim for an abuser's behavior. It's easier than you may think to give this message unintentionally. Reiterating the message "It's not your fault, but it is your opportunity to heal" can never be overemphasized.

DON'T try to help someone through their trauma beyond your capacity. Trauma can be very complicated and often requires specialized training.

DON'T minimize the potential impact of little-t trauma. Repeated minor injuries can have the effect of a thousand paper cuts.

DON'T focus your attention on condemning the source of the trauma. Focus instead on the job of healing.

DON'T gossip! Trauma experiences are very personal and demand the utmost confidentiality.

Suggestions

Here are three easy things you can do to aid your ability to help others struggling with trauma:

1. Investigate the availability of Christ-centered therapists in your area that are specifically trained in trauma, especially EMDR.

2. If you haven't already, open up about your own trauma experiences in an appropriate setting.

3. Read books such as *A Child Called It* to familiarize yourself with stories of those that have successfully survived trauma.

Chapter Seven

SHAME VS. GUILT

Guilt has gotten a bad reputation in recent years, but I believe it is a very valuable emotion. Guilt is feeling bad when you do something wrong. I want people to feel guilty. It means they know right from wrong. Guilt is what causes us to repent. When Peter gave the first Gospel sermon in Acts 2, announcing that Jesus was the Messiah the Jews had been anticipating and that they had crucified Him, "They were cut to the heart, and said to Peter and the rest of the apostles, 'Men *and* brethren, what shall we do?'" (Acts 2:37). They felt horribly guilty and were immediately wanting to know how to resolve that guilt. You're probably familiar with the cities in America that have removed the consequences for shoplifting and are therefore having stores leave town because of rampant theft. I would hope that most of us hearing these stories think to ourselves, "I would never steal just because the law changed; stealing is wrong." We would feel guilty about taking something we didn't pay for, and that guilt molds our behavior. If the only deterrent to bad behavior was the legal system, we would have anarchy. Thank God that most people still have the capacity for guilt.

Shame, on the other hand, is terribly destructive. Shame doesn't just say I did something wrong; it says I **am** something wrong. I'm broken, I'm flawed, I can't be fixed. While we are all sinners in need of a savior, I don't want anyone to get the impression they're unsalvageable or worthless. God loves us in our sinful state. Yet so many people get stuck in shame because of their past mistakes and remain burdened for years. God did not intend for us to live this way. You may know people that can't seem to forgive themselves for their past failures.

There are many factors that contribute to shame, and unfortunately the Church has been a major contributor for some people. I knew of a man that had been part of a very shame-based congregation that would frequently "dis-fellowship" people for their sinful behavior. When this gentleman was "dis-fellowshipped" due to a night of drunkenness, he was allowed to continue attending services but no one in the congregation, beyond the pastor, was allowed to speak to him or even acknowledge his existence! He just had to sit there as if he were a discarded piece of furniture and endure that shame until, after an arbitrary period of time, he was accepted back into the congregation, and everyone went on as if nothing happened! What a horribly shaming thing to have to live through.

I am glad to say I have never been part of a congregation that treated people that way. That kind of shaming is the polar opposite of how Jesus treated sinners. Think of the example of the woman at the well (John 4) or the woman caught in adultery (John 8). In fact, Jesus had some harsh criticism for the religious leaders that condemned Him for eating with sinners. Jesus made it clear He came to restore sinners, not burden them with shame (Mark 2:16-17). We shouldn't shoot our wounded, we should help them heal.

THE MYTH OF SELF-ESTEEM
So how do you help someone that seems stuck in shame? The first step in healing shame is to admit our guilt! Acknowledge that what we did was wrong, repent, clean up our mess and then change the way we behave in the future. The problem is some people do this but still feel unworthy. The issue is many get caught up in consulting their feelings about their own value. I read a brilliant essay by Dr. Christina Hibbert about the myth of self-esteem. The premise is that all efforts to gain a sense of value through self-esteem are destined to fail because we are basing our value on how we rank, how we feel about ourselves or how others see us. There will always be others that are more accomplished or "holier" than we are. Our feelings about ourselves are going to be up and down, often based on circumstances we can't control. Others aren't going to always approve of us, and those stuck in shame tend to focus on the people that think the least of them.

What we need instead is a sense of self-worth. An inner conviction that we have value, endowed to us by our creator, and that our failures don't define us. People that do continue to define themselves by their failures often suffer from what one person labeled "arrogant self-abasement." They view themselves as the worst of the worst. This is just as arrogant as thinking of yourself as the best of the best. You're neither! You're a unique, precious soul created by God with a free will, and you fall short just as everyone else does. The goal of life is not to be good enough as defined by some human standard or feeling, but to see ourselves through the eyes of our creator.

SEEING OURSELVES THROUGH GOD'S EYES
I was fortunate enough to have attended a Promise Keepers rally (remember those?) during which a professional athlete

described the first time God "spoke" to him. He described being a typical worldly guy before having a daughter, but after her birth he dedicated himself to being a devoted father. His daughter, however, came down with a devastating disease that left her severely cognitively impaired, to the point, he said, he went from wondering what college she might go to someday to wondering if she'd ever be potty trained. As he is pouring out his heart to God for his daughter, he said to God, "The worst thing is, no matter what I do for this little girl she will never know how much I truly love her." God's response was, "Yeah, I know; I have the same problem with you." We will never fully grasp the love of God this side of heaven, and that love isn't based on how close to perfect we are. His love was there before we were born, remained there at our worst moments, and will continue no matter what we do. Of course, He hurts when we go against His will, but His infinite love remains. This is the message those caught in shame need to hear. This is also the way we should love each other.

You're probably familiar with the different Greek words translated as "love" in the New Testament. When Jesus gives the new command to "love one another as I have loved you" in John 13:34, that word is "agape," or God-like love. It is a love that wants the best for the other person, regardless of feeling. That is how we can be asked to love our enemies; we can't always change our feelings about them but can choose to treat them lovingly. People stuck in shame need to treat themselves with agape love—want the best for themselves and see themselves the way God sees them. God doesn't focus on our flaws; He focuses on what He created. When a person caught in shame can embrace this, they can begin to grow into the fruitful Christians He designed them to be. When we encounter someone struggling with shame, we can show them that same God-like love and share with them how God has never stopped loving them more than they can imagine.

Sharing our own journey out of shame is an effective way to help those still stuck in it. Giving encouragement and genuine praise can be helpful, even if the person caught in shame doesn't initially believe you. I've also asked people that have difficulty with positive self-talk to write themselves a support letter. Just as you might write to encourage someone you care about that's feeling bad about themselves, I instruct them to write such a letter to themselves. Many have found this to be a good exercise in fostering a sense of self-worth.

DOs and DON'Ts

DO recognize the difference between shame and guilt.

DO call out shaming behavior in the Church whenever you see it.

DO praise God for the love He has shown to all of us!

DO love everyone as Jesus loved you, and encourage those stuck in shame to treat everyone lovingly, especially themselves.

DO see the value in everyone you meet, whether they see that value or not.

DON'T assume someone is going to get over their shame on their own. They may remain stuck for a long time.

DON'T ever fall victim to shaming anyone else. If you catch yourself condemning an individual, rather than a behavior, work to ensure them you and God still love them.

DON'T participate in the shaming of anyone by those around you.

DON'T look at anyone as unlovable. God may call on you to be the one to show that person His love.

DON'T minimize God's love for you!

Suggestions

Here are three easy things you can do to aid your ability to help others stuck in shame:

1. Formulate your own testimony of coming out of shame into grace.

2. Consider writing your own self-support letter. It's a rewarding exercise!

3. Take a moment and praise God for his endless love.

Chapter Eight

DEPRESSION/ANXIETY

A quick internet search will reveal that two of the most common mental health issues are depression and anxiety. Unfortunately, being a Christian does not exempt you from suffering either or both. While all of us feel sad or anxious, perhaps even frequently, some people have a more difficult time resolving emotional distress than others. Of all the definitions of depression I've heard, the easiest to understand and explain is "unreasonable or unaccountable despair." The sadness I feel is beyond reason or can't be accounted for by my life circumstances. It's feeling more than just sad about something that would make most people sad. The sadness has taken an inordinate amount of control in my life, and I don't know why. Depression may have a trigger or just arise seemingly out of nowhere. My efforts to resolve the sadness aren't working effectively and I'm feeling stuck.

For anxiety, the definition is similar: unreasonable or unaccountable fear. I'm overly focused on whatever has triggered my fear, beyond what others are likely to regard as reasonable. I may not even know what is triggering my anxiety, I just know I'm afraid and I can't make the fear go away. I may become annoyed by the fear because I know it doesn't make logical sense, but I can't seem to shake it. For many, the anxiety becomes self-perpetuating—they fear the emergence of their own fear.

CLINICAL VS. SITUATIONAL

There are two different types of depression and anxiety, based in large part on how your brain chemistry is working. Understanding which category a person is in can help you determine how to best help them. Clinical depression, in medical terms defined as a Major Depressive Disorder, usually refers to someone that has a true chemical imbalance in their brain. The neurotransmitters that are responsible for making us feel good aren't operating the way they do in most people. I may feel low energy regardless of the amount of sleep I've had, I may have little interest in things I used to get excited about, or I may find my attitude continually negative despite my desire to cheer myself up. One person described it this way: "It was like a veil would come down over me, without warning. I felt like I was on the verge of crying uncontrollably and I didn't know why. Sad things in the past would just pop into my mind, and I couldn't understand why I was thinking about those things; I'd already gone through them. It was like my emotional mind wasn't listening to my logical mind." The term "clinical" indicates that this category of depression is most likely going to require professional help and may need to be treated with medication. An estimate reported by Forbes indicates 8.4 percent of Americans have experienced a major depressive disorder. The most notable distinguishing factors are that the depression is there regardless of life circumstances, has physical features such as low energy, and is present most of the time.

IN THE CASE OF CLINICAL ANXIETY, IT LIKEWISE INDIcates fear or worry that goes beyond what circumstances warrant. I feel so much worry it keeps me from living a productive life. Even though I may know that the fear isn't sensible, the fear is there anyway and my efforts to ignore it aren't working. In some cases, I may have panic attacks, with actual physical symptoms such as a racing heart or sweaty palms. Anxiety disorders, diagnosed by professionals, include: Generalized Anxiety Disorders, Panic Disorders, Social Anxiety Disorders (fear particularly in social settings) and Specific Phobias. A friend shared with me an online article that he said explained his experience living with an anxiety disorder perfectly: "It feels like your mind tortures you. It gives you all these thoughts about what you should be scared of and horrible things that could happen to you. It tells you that you need to worry, analyze, and seek assurance about all these things…And yet, you worship your mind. You take what it says very seriously. You believe that if your mind says something, it must be important" ("Thoughts Are Just Thoughts: How To Stop Worshiping Your Anxious Mind" from Michael Stein, PsyD, 8/21/19). Indications are that more people suffer from an anxiety disorder at some time in their lives than with depression, though many suffer from both.

CONVERSELY, SITUATIONAL DEPRESSION OR ANXIETY indicates sadness or fear that comes as a response to some circumstance in life. A person that survives a car accident may have ongoing fears, especially when driving, though they have never had difficulties with anxiety in their past. A person going through a contentious divorce may experience such profound sadness that it interferes with their life, though they never had depression symptoms in the past. In these circumstances, professional help may still be necessary, but the focus is going to be more on the triggering event(s) and may involve trauma therapy, as discussed previously. People I've worked with that identify themselves as having situational depression or anxiety can easily identify the triggering event. They generally go back to the event when the fear or sadness rises, and they can't seem to get past it.

HOW TO BE HELPFUL RATHER THAN HARMFUL

So how do you help a person struggling with depression or anxiety? You can start by expressing your concern and your confidence they can achieve a sense of peace with God's help. It's not helpful to tell people to get over their depression or anxiety, but it is very helpful to declare healing is possible. People with mental health issues of any kind are likely to feel embarrassed talking about their struggles, so let them know you regard mental health concerns like any other health concerns—you're focused on how to heal.

If they're open to discussing their emotional responses, there are a number of ways anyone can help. Here are three items I've used that can be helpful. The first is a poem I learned long ago that is especially helpful for those with situational depression that still seem to be hanging on to past hurts:

> As a child, with a broken toy,
> comes for us to mend,
> I took my broken dreams to God
> because He was my friend.
> At last, I took them back and said,
> "How could you be slow?"
> He said, "My child, what could I do?
> You never did let go."

Giving people permission to let go of the pain or disappointment they've been holding on to can be very helpful.

The second is a simple analogy I've used numerous times for those struggling with anxiety. I compare it to a fire alarm going off in your home. Do you immediately go screaming out of the house yelling "call 911!" or do you check and see if someone burned toast? The fire alarm doesn't know the difference—it's just reacting to something in the environment. Those with anxiety disorders know their "alarms" are overly sensitive. They can't stop the alarm from going off, but they can choose how to respond.

The third involves the formula A + B − D = C, adapted from Rational Emotive Therapy, developed by Albert Ellis. It works like this: **A** is the **activating** circumstance. Someone gives us a compliment, someone insults us, we win $100, someone steals $100 from us. **C** is the emotional and behavioral **consequences** of that activator. We thank the person that complimented us, we insult the person that insulted us, we cheer winning the $100 or we key the car of the person that stole from us. People tend to think that **A = C**. If someone asked us why we keyed the car, we'd say, "Because they stole $100 from me." But that's not entirely true. If it were, every time $100 was stolen there would be a keyed car. There are a number of different options for how we respond, based in large part on the **B** in the equation above—our **beliefs** about how people should behave. I thank people when I'm complimented because I believe it's polite. I insult people that insult me because I believe in getting even. You get the idea. The **D** in this equation is to **dispute** your beliefs. Is it really Godly to get even with people? Is keying a car going to get me my $100 back? It's a simple formula that can help people focus on what's behind their emotional and behavioral responses. You can't change the activating circumstances that come your way, but you can control the consequences by disputing your beliefs, by trying to see things from another point of view. Thus, Activator + Beliefs − Disputing unhealthy beliefs = Consequences we feel good about. You can be a big help to people by working through their beliefs about a troublesome situation and how those beliefs shape their emotional responses.

Another way you can help is to recommend getting into some act of service. The number one assignment I have given to those stuck in depression is to do three nice things a day for someone else, preferably anonymously. Nothing makes you feel better than giving of yourself with no expectation of getting anything in return. You might still be sad—the prophet Jeremiah continued to weep even as he was doing what God asked him to do. Most people have told me that serving others took their focus off themselves, which gave them relief from their emotional burdens.

Finally, you can suggest the person struggling with anxiety or depression complete a gratitude list. Though it may sound cliché, I have found writing down specific ways I have been blessed to be very helpful in times of distress.

I've asked people to write out five things they're grateful for on a 3 X 5 card and carry it with them every day, then pull it out when emotions escalate. You can focus on your disappointments and fears too much, but I don't think you can ever focus too much attention on your blessings. When my daughter was very young, I taught her to pray by thanking God for anything she was grateful for. She would thank Him for things like her ceiling fan, her comforter, or anything else she saw in her room. It was a great lesson in the simple act of gratitude. She recognized the many good things that were in her life and was happy to express thanks for them. This simple attitude of thanksgiving is one I hope we never outgrow.

WHAT ABOUT MEDICATION?

You've likely seen commercials for the many medications available to treat depression. Some have voiced the belief that if you rely on God enough, mental health medication won't be necessary. I compare such thinking to the person that tells a diabetic God can heal them, so throw away their insulin. I myself was prescribed anti-psychotic medication after coming out of a drug-induced psychosis at age seventeen. Well-meaning people in A.A. told me I didn't need any of that crap, just go to meetings, read my Big Book, and talk to my sponsor. I did so, and promptly became psychotic again. My psychiatrist was really great. He said, "I understand you want to get off these pills, but right now I think you need them. You can tell me how they're working, and we can work together toward not needing them, but please don't go off them without telling me. We're on the same team." I wish everyone on mental health medication would have such a patient, understanding doctor. I know the struggles many have finding a psychiatrist they trust and can afford; some doctors seem to pull out the prescription pad as soon as they learn your name. Finding a Christian psychiatrist may be even more of a challenge. I am confident, however, in any congregation of any significant size there will be someone that has had a positive experience with medication for mental health issues. Hopefully you will be able to find such resources in your circle when you have the opportunity to help someone in need.

I am not a psychiatrist and have never been authorized to prescribe medications, but I have worked with hundreds of people on psychiatric medications and have a good idea of how they impact people. Here's my simple explanation of how I understand antidepressants to work: there are chemicals in your brain responsible for making you feel happy, two of which are serotonin and norepinephrine. When something happens that leads to happiness, your brain pumps out these chemicals and they get collected in buckets called receptors. After the happiness dies down, vacuums come and soak up the chemicals. Modern antidepressants don't make serotonin or norepinephrine, they slow down how fast your body soaks them back up. They are called serotonin or norepinephrine reuptake inhibitors. They give you better gas mileage for your brain chemicals. They usually do take some time to show a significant improvement, so those taking them usually have to wait a few weeks for maximum effect, but they can be very helpful for those with clinical depression. They are also increasingly being used to help with anxiety, though in my experience working with others the success rate seems to be inconsistent. For many years, the go-to medication for anxiety was benzodiazepines, such as Xanax or Klonopin. As an addiction counselor, I saw these drugs being abused on a regular basis, with very dangerous results.

There seems to be a growing amount of caution by medical professionals to prescribe these drugs as the addiction potential is so high, for which I am grateful.

There are, of course, those that will look to medication to change them without being willing to examine their own behavior. My quote is, "Don't look for a medical solution to a behavioral or emotional problem." If there's a medical need, there are medicines that may help. But no pill is going to erase self-pity if you're choosing to wallow in it, nor will it keep you from dwelling on your fears if you choose to dwell on them. Anyone wanting relief will have to make some changes and do some hard work. We can best help people by letting them know this and asking if they would like us to hold them accountable as they put in the effort. We can also ask them about their progress if they are taking medications, if they ask us to, though some people are reluctant to make it known they take pills. We can pray for people, along with encouraging them, and let them know the progress we see based on the efforts they put forth. As the late Fr. Joseph Martin stated, "Can prayer help with a toothache? Yes, if said on the way to the dentist's office."

DOs and DON'Ts

DO be inquisitive about a person's experience with their depression or anxiety. Most people I've worked with are happy to discuss what they're going through.

DO familiarize yourself with those in your life that have been successful in dealing with depression or anxiety.

DO share things that brighten your mood—songs, memes, funny stories, appropriate jokes, prayers, etc. Ask what brightens the other person's mood.

DO be solution focused. "What has worked for you?" is a more fruitful mindset than "What's wrong?"

DO smile! A happy face reflects joy. A look of worry and fear tends to produce the same in others. A preacher friend used to say, "Are you happy? Well, let your face know about it!."

DON'T stigmatize. A person struggling with mental health issues isn't flawed or abnormal any more than a person with diabetes. They have a condition that requires care.

DON'T tell them to just get over it. You don't **get over** any major issue in life, **you get through it**.

DON'T base progress on feelings. A person may still feel sad or fearful even if they're doing all they can to deal with their depression or anxiety. Progress is better measured by effort, not feelings that can't always be controlled.

DON'T be impatient. Depression and anxiety can be lifelong struggles for some.

Suggestions

1. Investigate stories of Christians finding relief from depression and anxiety.

2. Discuss how your congregation can bring awareness of the struggles some have with mental health concerns, like depression and anxiety, during Mental Health Awareness month (May 1 to May 31).

3. Spread the news about the Suicide Helpline number, 988.

Chapter Nine

GRIEF

I belong to a congregation in which the average age is somewhere in the 70s. As a result, we wind up having more funerals than baptisms. Grief is an issue that can't be avoided in the Church. Even Jesus, in the shortest verse in the Bible, wept for his friend Lazarus and his family though He knew He would be raising him from the dead. Experiencing grief is a natural part of mortal life and many deal with it in a positive, healthy manner. Others seem to stay stuck in grief and find their own lives diminished as a result. Those close to such people are sometimes at a loss as to how to be helpful, though they have a sincere desire to be of comfort.

GRIEF VS. MOURNING
The first thing to understand, when aiding those suffering from grief, is that there is a difference between grief and mourning. Grief is how we feel after a loss—missing the person, wondering how we will get along without them, remembering the times we spent with them and won't be able to spend any longer. We can experience grief whether or not an actual death has taken place. Those retiring can feel a loss after they stop working a job they've worked for years. When a friend moves out of state it's common to feel

grief. Any divorce situation can produce grief along with a myriad other emotions. Those negative emotions are a natural part of the healing process, and if expressed in a healthy way can be reconciled effectively.

Mourning, on the other hand, is what we do to express our grief: funerals, memorial gatherings, recalling stories about the person that is gone, activities done in a person's honor, etc. The problem is, for many, they feel grief, but they don't give themselves permission to fully mourn. I have seen far more pain resulting from people stuffing feelings of grief than from people seeking to express their grief through mourning. I've even seen people that have been told they should just get over it, or believe they are doing something wrong if feelings of grief persist.

Grief has no timetable, and there is no specific action for mourning that works for all people. The stages of grief (Kubler-Ross, 1969), originally designed as a way to help people deal with their own impending death, have sometimes been interpreted as a way of measuring if you're doing grief right, which is of little help. I tend, instead, to look at the five stages as a way to promote mourning effectively.

In the first stage, denial, the main dilemma is coming to grips with the loss rather than trying to run away from it. I'm told it's not uncommon, when a doctor has to tell a family member that their loved one didn't survive a medical procedure, for the family member to respond, "Just let me see them; I'm sure they'll be fine." If our emotional system isn't ready to accept the loss, not much healing is going to take place. While funerals are a place for many people to mourn, some describe feeling numb at a memorial service as they remain in denial. Others will focus on presenting a stoic demeanor, not wanting to let anyone see any cracks in their armor and denying their feelings of grief even though they outwardly acknowledge the loss. The best way out of this is to make the loss real in a way that's right for you, either writing a letter to the person that's gone, discussing the loss with those that can relate, or having a discussion at the grave. Someone coming to you for help that seems to still not have accepted a loss can be aided by a discussion on what method of acknowledging the death seems most appropriate to them.

In the second stage, anger, it's important to allow those experiencing a loss to be mad about it. While it's taboo to "speak ill of the dead," our feelings aren't bound by such rules. We may experience the emotional reaction of, "How could they leave me?" even if we rationally know such thoughts aren't warranted. We can be mad at doctors for not saving someone, even if they did all they could. Perhaps most destructively, we may be mad at ourselves for being the one that is still living when someone we cared about passes on. Trying to pretend like these emotions don't exist is likely to ensure they will continue under the surface. Pouring our heart out to God, as David often did in the Psalms, is much more effective than stuffing emotions.

In the third stage, bargaining, the job is to answer the question 'how will my life go on after this loss?' I try to help people in mourning formulate how they will honor the memory of the person that has passed on and to consider how their new life will look. The best eulogy I ever heard was at the funeral of a friend that had lost his mother. The preacher said, "Brothers and sisters, I did not come here to mourn today; I came to celebrate! When my son comes to visit me, I celebrate, because I'm glad to see him. When he goes back home, I celebrate again, because I know he's going to a good home. We can celebrate because our sister has gone to a good home!" In actuality, this preacher was mourning quite well, not with sadness but with a focus on the joy the person that passed is having in heaven along with a view ahead of how life will go on. I think many people would find the way the congregation I attend conducts memorial services quite peculiar. We typically have an open microphone for anyone that wants to tell a story of how they remember the person that has passed and how they envision remembering them in the future. There is frequently a great deal of laughter during this time, which is a great balance to the tears. Another example is a memorial area that some teens created in honor of a peer that was killed by a tornado while at a camp. That act of remembrance was a great healing activity for those teens.

The fourth stage is depression, and I believe the focus here should be on validating the mourner's emotions whenever they occur. I remember one individual wondering if something was wrong with them when they broke down in tears many months after a loss just because a song on the radio brought their loved one to mind. I reassured the person there is no expiration date on tears; you can't predict when grief will resurface, you can just make a commitment to effectively mourn whenever it occurs. The mourning process isn't meant to eliminate sadness, it is meant to allow us to go on with life after experiencing a loss.

Which leads us to the final stage, acceptance. The focus here is to get through our grief, not over it or around it. I like the term "reconcile" here. Think of your checkbook. When you reconcile it, you bring it back into balance. When you reach a level of acceptance after a loss, you have brought your life and your emotions back into a state of balance.

If you've been helping someone through their grief, it is very rewarding to see this balance come into shape. As mentioned, however, there is no timetable or order to these stages. So, you may be called on to help in the future if grief reappears even though it may seem to be reconciled today.

THE FISHBOWL AND LEXUS ANALOGIES

The best analogy I've ever seen about the grief/mourning process came from someone that worked at a program to aid children that have lost parents or other family members. She fills a large fishbowl with clear water and has several liquid food-coloring vials next to it. She asks the group what color their grief is. Someone might say, "Blue, I feel sad." She'll put a couple drops of blue coloring into the fishbowl. The water starts to turn color. Someone might say, "Yellow, I'm scared about going on with life without the person." She'll put in a couple drops of yellow. Fairly quickly, the water will become murky and dark. She then produces a bottle of bleach, and asks what people do to reconcile their grief. Someone might say, "Go to a grief group." She'll put in a bit of bleach. Someone else might say, "Write a letter to the person that's gone." She'll put in another bit of bleach. The water will begin to clear, but it will never become completely clear. The water is usually an interesting pastel color, but not totally clear. That is her point—loss changes us, and we have to deal with that change, but it doesn't have to be an unpleasant change. The new color of our life can be enjoyed, though we acknowledge it's different.

    I will give people this analogy: I'm going to give you a new Lexus. You have to maintain it and care for it, but it's yours for free. Someday I'm going to take it away, without warning. It might be in a day, it might be in six months, it might be in fifteen years. Do you still want it? I'm amazed at how many people say no, they'd grow too attached to it. It's a Lexus! Take the gift no matter how long you have it! If we can treat our relationships that way, appreciate them for as long as we have them and realize few will be permanent, we can approach the mourning process much more effectively. God has given us the gift of relationships in this mortal life. We can celebrate those that bless our life now and celebrate the memories of those that have blessed our life in the past, even while we mourn the losses that we must face.

GRIEFSHARE

While several in the Celebrate Recovery group I attend find support through the mourning process in that program, another Christ-centered program is GriefShare. Like DivorceCare, it is a 13-week, video-based support group that offers mutual support for those dealing with the loss of someone close to them. I live in a small city with several GriefShare groups available, so it's likely you'll be able to find one close to you.

ONE PARTICULARLY DIFFICULT ISSUE TO DEAL WITH IS the death of someone that is not in the Church. I have had multiple preachers tell me the most difficult task for them to do is to preach a funeral for a nonbelieving family member of someone in the Church. I am grateful to have never been called on to do so. I can't say I have an easy answer for how to aid someone dealing with such a loss, but I was witness to a perfect example of what NOT to do. A person of my acquaintance had such a loss, and at the memorial service brought some children in the family up front and told them the person that passed away wasn't in heaven, they were in hell and were going to live in torment forever. I have no idea what the person's motivation was for doing this, but it is clearly a grossly misguided response to the loss. The period of grieving/mourning is not the time for moralizing or condemnation; we can let God handle that. The time to discuss our mortality and our need for redemption is while we live. Jesus's admonition to people to give up all their worldly pursuits for a much greater reward in heaven was not given at a funeral. There is no sense in dismissing such verses in the Bible when someone has passed on without being in a saved state, but we can do so at the appropriate time and be compassionate with those that have suffered such a loss. Matthew 5:4 states, "Blessed *are* those who mourn, for they shall be comforted." Let's endeavor to be those that help provide such comfort.

DOs and DON'Ts

DO look for ways to remember and honor those that have passed on.

DO be compassionate, even if you do so without words.

DO share your fond memories of the person that has passed.

DO look for ways to discuss the future with the person that is mourning.

DO help prepare people for anniversaries, holidays, and other such times when grief may resurface.

DON'T give those that are grieving the impression they're doing it wrong; there's no set formula for getting through a loss.

DON'T assume someone is over their grief or expect them to be over it at some given time. Grief can come and go. Though it is likely to be less painful each time you have to go through a loss, the healing process has many ups and downs.

DON'T say, "I know just how you feel." You don't! You can certainly relate to people, and it is important to do so, but each person's experience of loss is uniquely their own.

DON'T be hesitant to express joy at a memorial service for someone that is now in heaven.

DON'T focus on the loss, but on what the future will look like.

Suggestions

Here are three easy things you can do to aid your ability to help others dealing with grief:

1. Investigate whether there is a GriefShare group in or near your congregation.

2. Celebrate all the relationships in your life and encourage others to do the same. Enjoy the Lexus while you have it!

3. Check in with the widows and widowers in your congregation. Let them know how much you appreciate them.

Chapter Ten

OTHER MENTAL HEALTH ISSUES

Depression and anxiety are just two of many mental health concerns people that come to you for help may be facing. The *Diagnostic and Statistical Manual of Mental Health Disorders*, fifth edition, the reference book for diagnosing mental health issues, lists over three hundred psychiatric diagnoses in twenty different categories. There are several considerations to be made in helping such people, including special concerns for particular categories.

In general, the main caution when dealing with those in the Church that struggle with mental health concerns is putting yourself in a position to give psychiatric or therapeutic advice beyond what you're qualified to give—much like a person with no medical training suggesting surgery for someone or suggesting a specific therapy or medication advice when they have no such training, which is inappropriate and potentially dangerous. It is much better to know of good resources to refer people to and support the efforts people have chosen to undertake. I have had many people ask me what they should do to help friends or family with mental health concerns, and I will encourage them to seek out competent professionals that either provide Christian counseling or are supportive of Christian viewpoints. I have also had to caution Church leaders from overstepping their bounds and asked them to consult professionals.

Another consideration for anyone helping someone with a mental health concern is to avoid approaching every issue as a "spiritual attack." I do believe that just as God is involved and concerned about all aspects of our life, the Devil is likewise actively engaged in trying to pull us away from God. Yet mental illness is just as real as cancer, emphysema, or any other health problem. Professionals that help with these concerns should never be supplanted by Christians that think they can just call on God to make the problem go away. We can look for ways to honor God in our efforts to respond to mental health concerns, and we can acknowledge our fight against evil, as in Ephesians 6:12— "For we do not wrestle against flesh and blood, but against principalities, against powers, against the rulers of the darkness of this age, against spiritual *hosts* of wickedness in the heavenly *places*." That being said, a person suffering from schizophrenia will be better served by a Christian-oriented psychiatrist than by an exorcist.

SCHIZOPHRENIA/PSYCHOSIS

I mentioned earlier in this book my suffering through a drug-induced psychosis when coming out of drug use in my late teens. It was terrifying; I didn't know what was real or not real, and the hallucinations I was having were extremely frightening. Psychotic disorders can plague anyone, but those that also have struggles with drug use are particularly vulnerable. The rates of psychotic disorders among those that use marijuana, particularly in their teens and early twenties while their brains are still developing, is much, much higher than among the general public.

Simply defined, schizophrenia involves interpreting reality abnormally. It can include hallucinations (seeing or hearing things other people don't see or hear, like the toaster talking to you or a voice in your head), delusions (believing something irrational, such as CIA agents monitoring your every move), severe paranoia or severely confused thought patterns. People struggling with schizophrenia struggle to know what's real and may respond to what they perceive in unusual or dangerous ways. A friend that has dealt with schizophrenia for years described having his first episode in his twenties while in the Navy. His schizophrenia was the paranoid type, and he began "thinking everyone was out to get me"; not a workable situation in the military. He now notes the critical importance, for him, to take his medication responsibly, have a good working relationship with his psychiatrist, and to practice calming techniques whenever possible. He has also learned to take appropriate time-outs when needed rather than to force himself to stay in high stress environments.

The movie *A Beautiful Mind*, the brilliant film by Ron Howard in which Russell Crowe depicts the very real struggles Nobel Prize-winning professor John Nash had with schizophrenia, is the best cinematic portrayal of the disorder I've ever seen. If you haven't seen the movie, **spoiler alert!** Nash has a reckless roommate, is approached by a government official that wants him to break codes, and sees a peculiar little girl, only to find out none of these individuals actually exist, they are hallucinations.

I use a particular scene in this movie to help those struggling with schizophrenia or other psychotic disorders: Nash gets help with his disorder but at one point quits taking his medication due to the side effects. His hallucinations return, to the point where he nearly drowns his infant daughter because of a hallucination's prompting. His wife heads out the door with the baby, but Nash stops her and says, "She never gets old," referring to the little girl. He was able to determine the hallucination wasn't real because the little girl never ages. In helping someone deal with a psychotic disorder, the most important thing to help them with is reality testing—determining what is real and what isn't. This can be more challenging than you might think; some people have regarded me as a potential enemy, because that's what their hallucination is telling them. People were patient with me as I worked to sort out reality from delusion during my psychosis; I've tried to be patient with others as they have tried to test reality themselves.

We can encourage people to try medications, but I would recommend against coming across as ordering them to do so. The same goes for encouraging therapy; some are afraid they'll get locked up or lose their job if people know about their psychosis, so they hesitate to seek professional help. I worked with an individual long ago that had several family members with schizophrenia; psychotic disorders have a strong genetic link, likely due to the passing on of the tendency for brain chemicals to operate differently. This individual was told by an aunt that had undergone several mental health commitments, "Don't ever tell anybody if you hear voices. They'll just lock you up." This poor man struggled in isolation with voices screaming in his head for years, trying to erase the voices with drugs, thinking he could never seek help. That is just one example of the horrible circumstances that may be facing people that come to you for help. Having an accepting posture and a willingness to listen without judgment may be challenging but is the best way to be of help. If they ask you what you think of their getting therapy, you can enthusiastically support such, but be cautious not to be seen as telling anyone they **must** seek therapy.

Schizophrenia is sometimes confused with what some call "multiple personalities," officially diagnosed as Dissociative Identity Disorder, or DID. The main component of this disorder is dissociation, having a period of time where you can't remember what happened. Similar to a blackout an alcoholic may have, in which they don't remember what happens while drunk though they continue to be functioning at some level, the person that dissociates stops recording information in their brain and, in the case of DID, they take on a different personality, one they won't remember when the period of dissociation ends. This condition is rare; I've only dealt with two such cases among the thousands of people I worked with. If you want further information on the disorder, you might want to try the book or movie *Cybil* about a real case of DID.

Some also associate schizophrenia with demon possession. This makes some sense, as the voices schizophrenics hear often take on an evil tone. But consider this: in examples of demon possession in the Bible, others could hear the voices too; Jesus and His disciples were even able to speak with them. In the case of hallucinations caused by schizophrenia, only the person with the condition can hear or see them.

Finding out more about the condition suffered by someone coming to you for help is advisable but be warned: looking up symptoms on the internet can easily lead to seeing a mental health disorder in anyone. It's like looking up the symptoms of lice on WebMD and suddenly feeling your head itch. I've found the best resource for understanding a person's mental health struggles is the person themselves. I've found most people willing and actually relieved to have the opportunity to talk to someone that truly wants to know how to help them. People that are successfully working on their schizophrenia can usually articulate how you can be of help to them.

NARCISSISM

There are several diagnoses in the DSM collectively referred to as "personality disorders," one of which is Narcissistic Personality Disorder. The name comes from Greek mythology. Narcissus was said to be the most beautiful of the gods, so beautiful that he fell in love with his own reflection in a body of water and froze there, staring at himself, until he was eventually turned into a flower. People with this disorder think of themselves as the center of the universe, and they have a hard time considering others as having their own universes. They are genuinely surprised when others don't see things as they see them. They become easily frustrated with people that question or challenge them, don't consider how their views could offend others and when they change their mind about something expect other people to change their minds as well. I heard a woman, when asked about "submitting" to her husband, say, "I'd submit to him if he'd do it right." Narcissists view themselves to be the arbiters of proper and improper, and never question themselves, at least not publicly. One person I met that struggles with narcissism described wanting others to do things his way, believing he always knew best. He also wanted validation on an almost constant basis and would become upset if he didn't receive it. You can see the kinds of problems this will produce in family relationships.

As with all personality disorders, one of the hallmarks is a lack of objectivity, an inability to see oneself through others' eyes. Narcissists aren't really concerned about this, as they're confident they're always right. Trying to help people with this or any personality disorder is a real challenge until you build up enough of a relationship with the person that you can gently explore with them an alternate point of view. There is a risk, of course, that the person will dismiss you in favor of someone that agrees with them. Narcissists tend to look for cosigners, not accountability partners.

You probably know people that are arrogant and overly sure of themselves but haven't reached the level of a full-blown narcissistic personality disorder. In such cases, discussing humility is very useful. The best story of humility I've heard comes from Mother Theresa: She was receiving a noteworthy award, as she did often for her charitable efforts, and an interviewer asked her if the accolades ever went to her head. Her response was to refer him to the occasion in the Bible when Jesus was entering Jerusalem on the back of a donkey as the crowd was singing His praises. She asked the interviewer if the donkey thought it was for him. Those with true humility will give thanks to God for any accomplishments they receive, knowing their abilities are a blessing from above. They are also able to recognize the contribution others have made in their successes and give credit for such. Humility is not thinking of yourself as less of a person, but thinking of yourself accurately, along with recognizing the value of others. I suspect many with narcissistic tendencies are secretly insecure, doubting themselves, but feel they must portray an air of overconfidence in order to sustain their self-image. I know I have greater respect for those that can admit their faults and can share honestly about how they've worked to resolve their personal defects. Sharing your own story of humble change, pointing out your admiration for people that can exhibit humility, and praising any humble change you see can be effective when trying to help a person that lacks objectivity.

One assignment you can give a person that truly wants to work on narcissistic tendencies is to thank one person a day for some contribution that person made to their life. Another is to identify one thing they learned or one thing they realized they were wrong about each day. This is a good exercise for anyone that wishes to gain humility and objectivity.

SOCIOPATHY

One of the most infamous mental health issues is sociopathy, diagnosed in the DSM V as Antisocial Personality Disorder. Shows about serial killers and those that appear to be blatantly evil get high ratings and many movies are made about people with this disorder. Simply put, a sociopath is someone that doesn't adhere to societal norms. They have little or no regard for the law, have no conscience that guides their behavior and have no empathy for others. Cities that have decriminalized theft have undoubtedly been very attractive to sociopaths; such cities have seen a proliferation of thefts perpetrated by relatively few individuals. I have used a simple "test" to see if someone has the mindset of a sociopath: A certain serial killer likes to attend the funerals of the people he kills. At one of these funerals, he meets a nice young lady and strikes up a conversation with her. After the funeral, he kills this lady's sister. Why did he do it? I'm told about 80 percent of sociopaths get the answer right away, while only 20 percent of the general public gets it. I got it right away when I first heard the test. Have you figured it out? He killed the sister so he could see the nice young woman at the funeral. That type of thinking is insane to most of us—technically, I suppose it is. But to a sociopath it makes sense, because it never occurs to them a nice young lady they had a good conversation with might not like having her sister killed. I had just one person I worked with over the years that I would regard as a true sociopath. He was proud of the fact that during the time he was involved in the program I worked in he had remained out of incarceration for five months in a row. It was the first time he had been out of confinement for five consecutive months since he was age eleven. After a short time, however, he came to me saying he was probably going back to prison. He described beating someone severely, and likely would have killed him if others hadn't held him back. I asked why he would do such a thing, and all he could say was, "The guy got in my face." When I asked why that would make him choose to nearly kill the guy, especially since he was on probation, he simply asked, "Well, what else would I do?" He truly couldn't formulate another response other than a brutal assault. His actions produced no remorse, guilt, or empathy.

The good news is, there are relatively few true sociopaths in the world, and they stand out like a sore thumb. They usually find themselves incarcerated and aren't likely to come to your congregation unless they think they can get something from you. What is much more common is someone that has learned to suppress their morals, and therefore act in ways that go against societal norms.

It may be helpful at this point to give an overview of Kohlberg's Stages of Moral Development. They proceed as follows:

1. Punishment/Reward—My idea of right and wrong is based on whether I'll be rewarded or punished. A two-year-old operates in this stage. I'll not get into my mom's things because I'll get in trouble, not because I respect her rules. I'll clean my room because I'll get a treat. This is the level sociopaths operate in. All two-year-olds are basically sociopaths. If you tell a toddler, "I'll give you a cookie if you put this poison in Aunt Ruth's coffee," Aunt Ruth is in trouble. They only know right and wrong because of what they get in the moment. This will not last long, however, much like a puppy that will stop peeing on the carpet if you punish him today but won't remember it tomorrow. Such a person might show up in your congregation if they hear you're giving out gas vouchers but will have no personal interest in spiritual values.

2. Reciprocal—My idea of right and wrong in this stage is still built on what I get, but I can be patient in the process. I don't need to get a reward right away; I'll keep my room clean all week in anticipation of a big reward at the end of the week. I'll give a classmate some of my colors because I know they have a lot of paper, and they'll give me some when I need it. It's still a self-centered value system, but I can wait for the reward. Some sociopaths have developed the

ability to put on a good face in order to get what they want. The Unabomber and Hannibal Lecter come to mind. Again, an adult that operates only at this level of moral development is going to stand out. Such a person might show up to your congregation if they're trying to get a job from an employer that attends there. There will likely be something that seems disingenuous about their presentation, and they'll move on when they get what they're after.

3. Good Boy/Bad Boy—In this stage, my idea of right and wrong is based on the values of those I admire. This is what you want with a child that looks up to you. Unfortunately, some people don't have a good role model to teach them morals growing up, so they wind up following the behavior and values of someone that exhibits immorality. I have worked with many people that have developed patterns of behavior that go against societal and legal standards because they were taught those patterns by unhealthy people. A couple of teens in Omaha were arrested when they posted a video of their prompting a young girl to use the most vile profanity imaginable while they laughed and encouraged her. The little girl didn't know she was doing anything wrong; she just knew the teens approved. Many gang members are recruited at a very young age because of this dynamic. They are vulnerable to being drawn in by a sense of camaraderie or family, and they have no stronger sense of morality at home that keeps them from the types of behavior gangs are famous for. An adult that operates in this level hasn't developed their own

set of values yet, they are following someone else's values without question. Such a person will show up to your congregation because their mother or other mentor said they should. At some point, if we are to be mature adults with our own set of morals, we will have to adopt our own value system.

4. Law and Order—In this stage, my sense of right and wrong is based on what is lawful and contributes to societal order (or at least my idea of what society should look like). This is usually a good thing, and leads to civility, but the problem that develops is the power of groupthink. If a strong voice in the group that you get your values from declares a behavior to be right or wrong, you'll go along with it. You can see this in any high school—students going against accepted standards because a few kids go against the rules and the group follows them. As I write this there is a story on the news about violence, looting, and chaos perpetrated by a large group of teens. If they see their friends engaged in this behavior, see minimal consequences, and have not developed an independent sense of right and wrong that stops them from such behavior, they're likely to do what the crowd does. An adult that can't (or won't) think for themselves is vulnerable to being manipulated by the group they're in. Such a person would come to your congregation with their group. In fact, a survey indicated that the most evangelical demographic measured was fourteen-year-old girls—when one in the group went to church, the whole pack went.

5. Individual Values—This is the point at which I develop my own set of values. Even if others I care about have a different point of view, I maintain my values because they are important to me. If you want to test this in yourself, think about important values you have, such as having a strong work ethic or keeping your house clean. If you discovered a friend had a different value system, e.g., they believe in doing the minimum to keep their job and don't mind a messy house, could you still be their friend? How about friends that have different political views than you? Can you discuss your differences politely and remain friends or would you demand they agree with you? We hope most adults develop independent values and can sustain civility with others of different values. Such a person will attend church because they believe it's an important part of their value system yet can calmly explain the reasons for their faith to a nonbeliever without judgment.

6. Universal Truth—This is the stage at which values and morals are based on the universal, spiritual principles that govern mankind. There is, of course, a lot of debate in the world about what those universal principles are, but some things are agreed upon by the vast majority of the civilized world: abusing an innocent victim is wrong, helping a vulnerable person in need is right. Those of us that agree with the Bible as the source of God's value system will devote ourselves to following those values. Such people attend worship services with the understanding that the world best operates in devotion to those Godly values.

True sociopaths will be very limited in their ability to advance through these stages of developing morals. Others, with the capacity for moral development, have become stuck, either because of poor mentoring or life circumstances that cause them to repeat immoral behavior. Just as you can get calluses on your hands from doing yard work over and over, you can get calluses on your morals by doing bad things over and over. A drug addict that shoplifts to afford a fix will probably feel bad the first time, but if he does so repeatedly, suddenly it doesn't hurt any more. A teen that vandalizes a business once for the thrill will hopefully regret this behavior the first time, but if this behavior isn't challenged and then repeated, they can get into a pattern of vandalism that doesn't appear to bother them.

So how do you help people that appear to have a deficiency in morals? As in the case of healing blisters you've developed during yard work, a person with calluses on their morals will have to soften their hearts and begin looking at how their behavior is impacting others. I believe most people can develop empathy if given the opportunity and encouragement to think of others. The Bible describes this as "Let nothing be done through selfish ambition or conceit, but in lowliness of mind let each esteem others better than himself" (Philippians 2:3). It would not have been commanded in scripture if God didn't think it could be done. I have seen many people that probably would have scared you in their former lives become genuinely caring, kind, morally upstanding people through God's power, and I've seen several go on to help others out of their morally deficient lives. You can patiently explain to someone that doesn't have your exact set of values why you believe the way you do and do so in a spirit of friendship rather than condemnation. I have found simply asking someone how they came to their value system to be fruitful; many have begun questioning their own values simply because I asked how those values developed.

ENTITLEMENT

I've reached the age where I get to start saying, "Kids today…" As a result, I'd like to share a few observations about the young people I've been privileged to work with over the past forty years and the changes I've seen in the mindset of many youth I've encountered. The most concerning trend I've seen in recent years is the tendency for many young people to think they are entitled to certain privileges without having to earn them. I actually had a twenty-seven-year-old sit in my office and say, "I don't think I'm ready to adult yet." I was aghast! He didn't say, "I don't think I'm ready to eat this week," or "I don't think I'm ready to have a roof over my head," he just didn't think he was ready to take on adult responsibilities. He wanted someone else to take care of him for a little while longer. This was the polar opposite of the attitude I had in my late teens. When I had the opportunity to move out on my own at age nineteen and start paying my own bills, having my own freedom, I welcomed the challenge. Too many young adults I've encountered simply don't see any benefit to being self-reliant.

I can accept the young person that doesn't know how to take care of themselves, and I can understand the parent that struggles to encourage their teen to start taking on adult responsibility. However, the rampant examples of people in their twenties and thirties that are happy to sleep on mommy and daddy's couch, work part-time at a fast-food restaurant, spend all they earn on video games and junk food, have no plan for how they are going to support themselves, and act as though they will be sixteen forever is astounding. I actually had a person I worked with, living at home with no plan to move out, say, "It's my parent's responsibility to provide a home for me as long as they can." He was forty-six!

I could go on and on about the proliferation of government handouts and enabling parents that have contributed to this phenomenon, but the focus of this book is on helping. So how can you help a young adult that wants to stay a teenager or a parent that is reluctant to let their baby grow up? As I mentioned in the codependency chapter, stopping enabling is an essential first step. If a parent is coming to you not knowing what to do about their twenty-year-old still living at home, simply ask them what the move-out plan is. If you hear a bunch of excuses, you'll need to be firm in letting them know their twenty-year-old needs to struggle before they can fly. Focus on them helping the twenty-year-old develop a self-reliant mindset. Have the twenty-year-old, not the parent, set a list of tasks each day (put in ten new applications each day, volunteer in a career field they're interested in, etc.) and hold them accountable for completing the tasks. If a young person comes to you for help in taking on adult responsibilities, the principles of encouragement and accountability also apply. There is likely someone in your congregation that would be happy to hire a dependable young person in need. Again, you don't aid anyone by doing the work for them. If I go to the gym and work out for you, it's not going to make you any more fit. But coming up alongside someone that wants to better themselves may be the difference between success and failure.

I have heard parents voice concerns about their children's feelings when they want to encourage them to be more responsible. I heard a preacher give a great example of how to handle this. He said, "I told my son to take out the garbage. He said, 'I don't feel like taking out the garbage.' So, I told him, 'I can change how you feel.' He didn't need to do it when he felt like it, he needed to do it when Daddy said so." I certainly haven't always felt like doing a difficult job, but I did it because I knew it was the right thing to do. Our feelings sometimes give us terrible advice about what the right choice is. We can help young adults and their parents sort out the right decisions rather than look at just what feels right.

Tom Peters, author of *In Search of Excellence*, gave an excellent lecture in which he asked the question "What ever happened to good customer service?" No one even seems to expect it anymore. When you're at a fast-food restaurant and a seventeen-year-old who couldn't care less messes up your order, if you say something about it people in line around you will look at you as if to say, "Who are you to expect average service?" The good news is, if you provide quality, friendly service and work hard every day, people will seek you out and flock to your place of business, paying whatever you ask, and it won't cost you a dime extra. This is the attitude you want to instill in any young person, especially your own children. If you're helping a parent of a young person that has no interest in doing the work of being an adult, explore how they can gently but firmly make it uncomfortable for their child to continue taking advantage of their parent's care.

NAMI

One of the best resources I've come across in dealing with mental health issues is the National Alliance on Mental Illness, or NAMI. They describe themselves as "the nation's largest grassroots mental health organization dedicated to building better lives for the millions of Americans affected by mental illness." Their website has a number of resources, including educational material, information for family members, and support group information. I spoke with a NAMI representative on their hotline. She described their wealth of referral information for therapists and programs in any area, specific information on faith-based providers upon request, NAMI support groups referral information for family members, and referrals to mental health crisis centers. Though she noted the importance of calling 911 or 988 in true emergency situations, she indicated that NAMI representatives can help callers determine the appropriate next step in a time of crisis. Getting in touch with NAMI can be beneficial for anyone dealing with a mental health issue. Likewise, Celebrate Recovery is dedicated to helping those struggling with mental health concerns, just as they help with any hurt, hang-up or habit. Many Celebrate Recovery groups have a person devoted to engaging those that struggle with mental health issues.

DOs and DON'Ts

DO listen to those seeking help for mental health issues as they describe their experiences. Showing true interest may be one of the most helpful things you do.

DO give one of the tools above a try or use similar analogies you've seen work. The simpler the tool, the better.

DO celebrate successes.

DO exhibit an attitude of gratitude and foster such an attitude in others.

DO look for opportunities to foster responsibility in young adults, such as giving them service opportunities in your congregation.

DON'T stigmatize. People with mental health issues aren't "those people"; they're people that just happen to have those issues.

DON'T abandon your boundaries when working with people that exhibit moral deficits. You don't help anyone by letting them take advantage of you.

DON'T project your opinion for or against medication onto someone with a different opinion. Simply state your view and allow them to have their view.

DON'T try to diagnose someone based on symptoms you find on the internet! If there are legitimate concerns, let a professional determine if a diagnosis exists and how to best address it.

DON'T gossip. It can be tempting to discuss people's issues with others, but you can do a great deal of damage by breaking a confidence.

Suggestions

Here are three easy things you can do to aid your ability to help others dealing with mental health issues:

1. Contact NAMI about what they offer and resources they are aware of in your area.

2. As mentioned in a previous chapter, plan an event during Mental Health Awareness month in your congregation to increase awareness.

3. Share about any mental health issues you've struggled with, especially the successes you may have had.

Chapter Eleven

DISABILITIES

My wife is disabled and has been in a wheelchair virtually all her life. Here's a brief synopsis of her story in her own words: "I was born in a small, rural Midwestern community. I was born with spina bifida, which is a birth defect that caused me to have a sack of fluid outside my lower spine and required surgeries to close my back and have a shunt put in to keep spinal fluid from collecting around my brain. I have no ability to use my legs and they won't support my weight. As a small child I was in and out of hospitals, with many surgeries. I briefly walked with braces that went up to my waist and crutches that went under my armpits, until my hips went out of their sockets multiple times. It was such a chore to get from point A to point B, I didn't care about point B anymore. Eventually, a doctor said I'd be much better off in a wheelchair, and I was grateful to have him say so. I attended kindergarten in that small town but was homeschooled for the next year as the local school wasn't accessible. My parents knew they wouldn't be able to care for me at home full time. They then learned of a school connected to a live-in institution for disabled children in Omaha, Nebraska. As the residence was only open weekdays and my parents were so far away, I lived with foster families on the weekends from second grade through high school. I'd go back with my family in the summers and during school breaks of at least a week. Back in those days, most people, including many doctors, had a very limited idea about what people with disabilities would be able to do. Resources back then were not what they are today. Accessibility was limited and many people seemed to think those with disabilities would be happier 'with their own kind'; at the time, I didn't know any better. The school I attended was good for me at the time, I thought. I had a few really good friends, including my best friend from second grade until the day she died when I was in my thirties. When I was transitioned to a local public high school I just did what I had to do to finish; I didn't really have any friends and I felt like a nobody. I did have a few people use my disability to get a tardy excuse by pushing me from class to class. After high school I had a bit of a dilemma: I discussed with my caseworker some unhappiness I had with my foster family, and it got back to my foster mother. This led to me eventually getting my own apartment, designed for people with disabilities, which I then lived in for thirty-two years. I led a pretty solitary life, and became a junk-food junky. One day I hit the bottom of a bag of chips and began to cry. I prayed to the Lord, 'I can't stop this bad habit by myself. If I'm going to get a handle on this, I'm going to need your help.' A short time later, I had a problem with my shunt, which I discovered only after waking up in the hospital with part of my head shaved. I found out from my home-health aide I had been complaining of terrible headaches for a week; when I woke up in the hospital, I had no memory of that week or the pain. The doctors also referred me to a dietitian, and I started on a healthy food program and eventually began utilizing physical therapy equipment three days a week. After a while, I realized how well it was working and I remembered my prayer. I started doing internet searches on Bible studies. I had been raised Catholic, though I was never really involved as an adult in the Catholic church. I came across a study from the Church of Christ, which sounded a lot to me like the Church of the Bible, and I started praying that God would give me an opportunity to start attending somewhere. I called a local congregation, asking if they had a way I could get to services, as the accessible bus system in town was not available in my neighborhood on Sundays. Somebody from the congregation was able to provide me with transportation and seven weeks later I was baptized, with the help of several people. I continued Bible studies with the preacher at this congregation for about three years and started attending a singles group. I met my husband, the author of this book, soon after. There was a point in my life I wondered if I would have been better in social situations if I had been mainstreamed earlier in my school career; but now I'm thinking that if anything had been done differently, my life wouldn't be what it is today. I believe that everything I've been through and all the decisions that my parents made for me brought me to where I am in my life and made me the person I am today. I can't imagine a life where I am more at peace and happier than I am now."

When I met my wife in the abovementioned singles group, I thought she was a fascinating human being, with a beautiful smile and the sweetest disposition I'd ever seen. When we started dating, I wrote the first of many poems for her:

> Seems the chair is the first thing most folks notice
> And I'm sure some never look much closer, to see the person there
> The first thing that caught my eye was her smile
> that lit up the room, and displayed a sense of warmth, concern, and care
> I took the time to get to know her better
> I have been so blessed for doing so
> I've come to know the loving soul I'm proud to call my friend
> And my life has been enriched more than you'll know
> She's heaven on wheels; that chair's not who she is
> It's just how she gets around
> Take some time and get to know her, and I'm sure you'll see
> She's the closest thing to an angel to be found.

I have learned so much about the experience of being disabled in the years since then. As my wife says, "It's not a fate worse than death. No matter what your lot in life is, you can make it worse or better based on your attitude. Nobody's going to want to be around a person that mopes all day, so if you want to add loneliness to your problems, have a negative attitude. If you have a positive attitude, you'll draw more people to you." I can attest to how terrific her attitude is. She is almost continually grateful, and is willing to put up with me, which is angelic by itself.

I've discovered that "attitude" is an aeronautical term, referring to the balance of a plane in its relation to the ground. If you think of your personal attitude as your ability to balance all your life circumstances with your foundational values, your attitude will be more likely to be positive.

Though disabilities vary wildly, I can think of several important considerations when trying to help someone that is disabled or those that care for them. The most important thing is to see the person not as their disability but as a precious individual with a unique struggle. Try not to assume what their capabilities are without investigation. My wife had an illustrative situation once while volunteering at a Special Olympics events: a person came up to her and started talking to her as if she had a cognitive deficit, talking to her like a child, simply because she was at this event in a wheelchair. When my wife responded like the college-educated adult she is, the person was taken aback and seemed a little embarrassed.

Also, address the person directly when possible. My wife has had waitstaff at restaurants ask me or someone else she was with what she was ordering, not her. She's had to pipe up and announce she can order for herself. You'd be amazed how quickly you can engage a disabled person if you simply notice they are there. This is a common principle to follow when talking with a deaf person that uses an interpreter—even if the person can't hear you, you look at them rather than the interpreter. Much of what you're communicating comes through nonverbal cues. If a disabled person isn't able to interact with you and a caregiver steps in, make every effort to acknowledge the individual.

Accessibility in your congregation is also something to consider, including home Bible studies or get-togethers in homes that may not be accessible. For example, we sit up front because when people stand to sing or pray my wife can't see the screen. Be sure you have space for someone in a wheelchair, devices for those that are hearing impaired, know of interpreters for those that are deaf, and have any other accessibility items that can make your congregation more inviting for those with disabilities. If you're not sure, ask the person in need. If you're out in public, be sure not to park in handicapped spaces if you're not authorized to do so. Don't park blocking curb cutouts or access lanes beside handicapped spots marked by diagonal lines. Don't use restroom stalls designated for handicapped people if there are other stalls available. These simple acts of courtesy will be noticed by anyone that needs those accommodations. The important thing is to help the person with a disability as an individual, not just focus on the disability itself.

My wife was born with her disability, but some sustain their disability through illness, accidents, or other life-changing events. This is likely to produce some level of trauma and possible depression; the chapters devoted to those issues would apply in those situations. There are also those that suffer limitations through their own bad choices, such as several I've worked with that have life-changing injuries (amputations, brain damage, etc.) due to their addictions. Whether the person caused the disability or not, they may experience a great deal of self-pity and have little hope they'll be able to get out of it. The people I've worked with learned not to say, "Why me?" because I would consistently share with them the words to the song "Why me, Lord?" by Kris Kristofferson, which begins "Why me Lord? What have I ever done to deserve even one of the pleasures I've known?" Most of the things that happen that are beyond our control are awesome! The sun came up this morning without my doing a thing to make it happen. The atmosphere protects the earth from objects in space that could destroy us all. I was born in the greatest country there is, in my opinion, through no work on my part. I could go on and on. Yes, we sometimes suffer from the sinful behavior of others; yes, devastating things can happen to us seemingly at random. But we also have countless positive things happen in our lives, if we're willing to look for them, and we can sing God's praises no matter what our struggles may be. A book that deals with this well is C.S. Lewis's *The Problem of Pain* (2015). He makes a compelling argument for sustaining our faith through our strife.

FAMILIES, LIKEWISE, CAN STRUGGLE WITH CAREGIVING, although I've actually encountered more people "over-helping." We have a manual ramp hooked up to our van to get my wife in and out, and I put it up and down with no more thought than you do shutting your car door when you get out. Several times people have asked me, "Can I help you with that?" and I've answered, "With what?" before realizing they're talking about the ramp. I am sure there are those that are burdened with the amount of care they provide and are hesitant to cast that burden on others. One of the skills those with disabilities need to learn is how to fend for themselves within their abilities and to assertively ask for help when needed. Similarly, family members and caregivers need to know their limitations, get training when they can provide care, and seek aid when the need is beyond their ability. We as potential helpers can offer our aid when requested, without interjecting ourselves into someone else's process. There are times my wife needs someone to open a door if I'm not around; there are other times she can get it herself. If she needs help, she'll ask. It's nice when someone offers, but it can come off demeaning to assume someone with a disability can't do something until they tell you they can't.

Especially in the case of a disability acquired later in life, the trauma and depression can afflict family members as well. It can be a real challenge in a marriage if my mate, whom I had counted on to share our golden years, suddenly has some serious limits to what they can do. Grieving the loss of the dream I had may take a while. As mentioned with several other issues, gratitude is a valuable tool. When Paul says, in Philippians 4:11–13, "Not that I speak in regard to need, for I have learned in whatever state I am, to be content: I know how to be abased, and I know how to abound. Everywhere and in all things, I have learned both to be full and to be hungry, both to abound and to suffer need. I can do all things through Christ who strengthens me," I don't think he intended to leave a disability out of the equation. Christ accounted for any struggle we have or will face, physical or mental, long before we were born and will give us a path to bring glory to His name within the abilities we or someone we care for may have.

There's a famous story from the late great Paul Harvey that exemplifies the value anyone, despite their limitations can have in bringing glory to God. The story goes something like this: a teacher sent her class out on a bright spring morning to find examples of springtime and put them in little plastic eggs, then present them to the class. One student had a twig with a bud on it in her egg. Another had a small feather from a robin. Then little Johnnie came up front. The teacher was concerned, because Johnnie suffered from physical and mental maladies that made him a little slower than the other children. Johnnie opened his egg, and it was empty! The teacher tried to usher him back to his seat, thinking he hadn't understood the assignment, but Johnnie spoke up and said, "No, no! My egg is empty because the tomb is empty. And I know I have eternal life because the tomb is empty." A short time later, Johnnie's maladies took his life. At his funeral, his classmates didn't bring flowers to put in his casket, but little, empty plastic eggs.

That little boy, who many may have thought would never have much of an impact on the world, gave a terrific message about the resurrection that has been told to thousands and thousands of people. No matter what the disability of the person you're working with, or the struggles family members or caregivers may have in serving them, know that God can use those struggles to forward His purpose. James 1:2-4 states, "My brethren, count it all joy when you fall into various trials, knowing that the testing of your faith produces patience. But let patience have *its* perfect work, that you may be perfect and complete, lacking nothing." You wouldn't be the person God is now molding you into without going through the trials you've had to face. May he use those trials to give you a powerful message. This is the attitude you want to encourage in those dealing with disabilities.

DOs and DON'Ts

DO assess the ways in which your congregation is accessible and inviting to those with disabilities; make changes where appropriate.

DO engage those with disabilities as you would anyone else.

DO encourage family members and caregivers to care for themselves and seek assistance when they need it.

DO ask how you can help a disabled person that seems to be in need of aid; don't assume you know what they need.

DO fight self-pity with gratitude!

DON'T talk to the nondisabled person with a disabled person about what that person might need; talk to the disabled person directly.

DON'T use services designated for the disabled. They need those services to fully function, you don't!

DON'T dismiss the abilities of those with limitations. My wife is a very dedicated servant in sorting mailings and stuffing envelopes for a missionary preacher that sends out thousands of Bible lessons.

DON'T "talk down" to a person in a wheelchair, talk to them like an intelligent adult. It's better to talk over someone's head and have to adjust than to talk to someone like a child and offend their intelligence.

DON'T always assume a disability is an insurmountable barrier. There are innumerable assistive devices and technologies that can provide opportunities in many situations.

Suggestions

Here are three easy things you can do to aid your ability to help others dealing with disabilities:

1. Check out the Paralympics (for people with physical limitations) or Special Olympics (for people with cognitive disabilities). The athletes are truly inspiring, and the competition is fun to watch!

2. Listen to the stories of those that have dealt with disabilities and maintained a positive attitude.

3. When in doubt about how to help someone, ask them.

Chapter Twelve

FINAL THOUGHTS

The Bible indicates, in John 13:35, "By this all will know that you are My disciples, if you have love for one another." This is the agape, God-like love that any of us can exhibit to a person in need and brings out the best in all of us. The qualities others see in us as we serve others are summed up in the fruits of the Spirit (Galatians 5:22-23).

Love—there is no greater love than when we serve each other. Jesus gave his disciples the command to love one another in the same chapter that described His washing the disciples' feet. In the movie *Jesus Revolution* **spoiler alert!** there is a scene in which the formerly stuffy preacher, after receiving complaints from his usual members about the "hippies" coming to services in bare feet, chose to remedy the situation by washing the hippies' feet. What a terrific example of showing humble love and taking away an opportunity for the traditionalists to judge.

Joy—If you're not having fun serving others, you're doing it wrong! Though I've had several heartbreaks and disappointments in my career helping people through their most difficult times, I've also had more joy than you can imagine. Seeing someone achieve freedom from their issues is beyond rewarding. Psalm 100:2 tells us to "Serve the Lord with gladness."

Peace—I've written a lot about being a solid rock in a river of chaos. You can best do this by sustaining a peaceful stance. Of course, this will mean being at peace in your day-to-day life. Taking appropriate care of yourself is part of the process in serving others.

Patience—The NKJV renders this "long-suffering." Helping others through their issues is usually not a sprint, but a marathon. There are few quick fixes but many long hauls in working through addictions, family problems, mental health issues, or the other problems described above. Exhibiting calm patience can be very inspiring to those that are in a state of panic.

Kindness—The term "random acts of kindness" has been around for decades, to the point there is now a National Random Acts of Kindness Day. We can all do something to benefit others every day, and thus inspire others to help others, starting a chain of charity that continues indefinitely. In my own life there are specific little acts of kindness that have had an enormous positive impact on me; I'm sure you can think of such acts that had a profound impact on you. Strive to be that person for someone else.

Goodness—Contrary to the beliefs of relativists that believe right-and-wrong is an individual decision, there is a standard of good and evil. God is the source of good and bad, not our opinions and feelings. We need never shrink from calling a sin a sin, doing so without shame or judgment but with humility and honest discernment. We aid others by living according to biblical standards of right and wrong, admitting when we go against those standards and striving to live more closely to God's standard of goodness.

Faithfulness—Steadfastness and loyalty are synonyms. We stick by those we are trying to help, not just pat them on the head and go on our way. I have been so enriched through the process of sponsorship and mutual support. Those that were faithful in dedicating themselves to helping others have inspired me to be faithful in helping those I serve. May you be so inspired in helping those you serve.

Gentleness—Restoring people gently (Galatians 6:1) can often be tedious and painstaking. It can often seem tempting to vent our frustration or blast people with admonishment in a harsh and demeaning manner. Jesus cleansing the temple was a blistering example of the need we have, at times, to speak loudly and bravely. Yet the love of God we express toward those that are hurting needs to be gentle, following Jesus's example of gentleness in dealing with those that are repentant. Philippians 4:5: "Let your gentleness be known to all men. The Lord *is* at hand." A principle to follow is if you must admonish someone, do so in private. If you are able to praise someone, do so publicly.

Self-control—Also translated "temperance," this is the quality of keeping our negative impulses in check. As a fruit of the Spirit, it is obvious we won't be able to just grind our teeth and be perfect, we'll need God's help. Part of helping others is sharing how God has enabled us to have success in the battle with our sinful nature.

I OFTEN HEAR FROM THOSE THAT ARE STRUGGLING HOW much they feel like they have no purpose in life. While aiding others in need may not be the only thing that gives you a sense of fulfillment, it sure beats feeling like you contribute nothing to the world. There is a developmental theory that can be useful in establishing a sense of purpose.

It comes from Erik Erikson, and the unique perspective of his theory is that it follows development throughout our lifespan rather than just outlining development into adulthood. In each stage he identifies a conflict that must be mastered to produce effective psychological well-being. I'd like to present the stages, along with ways we can aid people in each stage.

Trust vs. Mistrust—This occurs in infancy, and involves a baby being able to feel safe and secure in their environment. I unfortunately have worked with those that weren't able to develop a sense of security in infancy. This can produce a condition known as Reactive Attachment Disorder and leads to serious difficulties in bonding with others. If you are dealing with a person that suffers from this difficulty, you can slowly but consistently build a bond with them. Sunday school teachers can be especially effective in building these bonds. Working with parents, especially foster or adoptive parents, you can encourage them to be gentle and patient in the bonding process. Just like being patient as you wait for a bunny to eat out your hand, you can encourage parents or caregivers to take small, gentle steps in building trust.

Autonomy vs. Self-Doubt—This occurs with toddlers as they learn to do things for themselves. When I was this age, my parents made audio recordings of me. One of my favorite sayings at that age was, "Me do it!" I took great pride in being able to dress myself and accomplish something through my own effort. Children that are treated too critically may have their sense of initiative squelched; children that have too much free rein may develop a lack of concern about the impact of their behavior on others. A coworker had a couple come into her office complaining that their child ruled the house, and they couldn't do anything to control him. The child was two! Obviously, these parents hadn't learned that balance of encouraging autonomy (meaning "self-governing") while setting appropriate limits. Simple techniques like giving a toddler a choice of three outfits to wear or three options for lunch can help achieve this balance. In Colossians 3:21 fathers are warned, "Fathers, do not provoke your children, lest they become discouraged." We can be encouraging while setting responsible, Godly limits.

Initiative vs. Guilt—This occurs in the preschool years. A lot of shame is developed in these years, and usually stems from young children feeling everything they do is wrong. Some carry this to a sense that they themselves are wrong and will never be worthwhile. A simple habit you can encourage parents to get into is praising their children for some accomplishment every day. They say it takes ten "at-a-boys" to make up for one "you idiot." The process of training up a child in the way they should go isn't purely about doling out punishment or recognizing flaws, it's about teaching and modeling success in living a Godly life. This will involve correction but also involves reassurance of God's love, despite any mistakes we make, and a focus on the sinful behavior rather than a flaw in the individual.

Industry vs. Inferiority—This occurs in elementary school. I experienced my share of bullying during these years, and I remember experiencing more fear than peace. I would hope all of our congregations are safe environments for children to grow in their love of God and understanding of scripture, promoting their productivity and value. Unfortunately, parents are often battling against the emotional and sometimes physical assaults their children experience in school. The first people you will help through their struggles will likely be your children. As parents, guardians, or concerned extended family we can take a true interest in the experience of grade-schoolers and work to instill in them a sense of capability. I was a YMCA basketball coach for a group of third to fifth graders. It was such a joy to encourage their development in a safe, fun environment. I am convinced that sports involvement can be transformational at this age if children find the sport enjoyable and they can develop a sense of productivity. I would rather have young men get out their aggression on a football field than in a gang fight. I wasn't a very good athlete at that age and certainly felt inferior. Having an adult that encouraged me to develop and use my limited talents would have really helped. Look for opportunities to be a source of encouragement for a youngster feeling inferior.

Identity vs. Role Confusion—This happens in adolescence when we start to develop our sense of personal identity. Just look at all the problems teens have with their identities today! Even once basic things like gender have become sources of confusion. Many adolescents struggle with competing messages. Parents, friends, social media, teachers, and other sources flood young minds with conflicting ideas of what's right, what's wrong, what's permissible and what's inappropriate. Parents naturally feel their influence over their teens slipping and worry about the choices they'll make. As the dilemma indicates, the challenge is for the young person to find their identity in Christ. While the time to force this on a child has passed by this age, there are plenty of ways we can support and encourage those in this stage of development as they become the adults

God designed them to be. My daughter found Bible camps and youth rallies to be very positive influences at this age. I was very grateful when a teen in a Sunday school class I teach said he appreciated my talking to him like an adult; I've found this to be the best stance when teaching or talking things through with a teen. Most teens have already done a lot of thinking about their identity and are aware of the pitfalls facing them. Having a discussion on equal footing is likely to be more productive than talking down to them. Helping parents to avoid power struggles and to develop a more adult-to-adult relationship with their teens is another way to assist families dealing with adolescent role confusion.

Intimacy vs. Isolation—This describes young adults (19 to 40) that are often deciding on a mate and building long-lasting adult friends. Sadly, this is also the age when many young adults leave the Church. Most of the people I've worked with over the years were in this stage, and most described few truly intimate relationships. They seemed to have trouble knowing how to really love others. By loving such people unselfishly we can model what healthy friendship looks like. Rather than trying to steer people in this stage to "the right person," I think it's more useful to guide them to the right ways to love others. The book *I Kissed Dating Goodbye*, by Josh Harris (2003), provides a great description of the benefits of adopting the principles of courting, getting to know a prospective mate fully rather than simply looking for a quick, feel-good, temporary encounter. Compare this to trying to find a satisfying intimate relationship through an online app or at a singles bar. There are huge congregations in the world that do really well in incorporating programs and groups that give young adults the chance to make connections with other believers. When this is coupled with sound biblical truth, any congregation will flourish.

Generativity vs. Stagnation—This is what we describe as "middle age" and is the time to determine our level of contribution to the world. I have come to the end of a four-decade-long career in helping others and can look back with contentment. There are those that look back in this stage and don't like what they see—either they're disappointed by their career choices, haven't been as successful financially as they planned, or they are disappointed by their marital/relationship history. The biggest challenge in this stage is that time is running out. I believe the nature of what is referred to as a "mid-life crisis" has to do with this realization. I've found focusing on serving others is crucial in this stage. Simply looking at financial or business success is rarely fruitful. In fact, some of the richest people I know suffer the greatest amount of self-doubt. None of the apostles got their satisfaction from being great fishermen or tax collectors, they got their satisfaction from serving in the Kingdom. Sharing the satisfaction we receive from serving can be the most effective way to help those feeling stagnation.

Integrity vs. Despair—We come to the end of our life and either feel good about what we've accomplished or despair that we've wasted the life God gave us. I have encountered people with objectively more years left in their lives that still despair they have blown it, their lives are a complete disappointment. As long as we draw breath there is time to do God's work. Look at the example of Simeon in Luke 2: "And behold, there was a man in Jerusalem whose name *was* Simeon, and this man *was* just and devout, waiting for the Consolation of Israel, and the Holy Spirit was upon him.

And it had been revealed to him by the Holy Spirit that he would not see death before he had seen the Lord's Christ. So, he came by the Spirit into the temple. And when the parents brought in the Child Jesus, to do for Him according to the custom of the law, he took Him up in his arms and blessed God and said: 'Lord, now You are letting Your servant depart in peace, According to Your word; For my eyes have seen Your salvation which You have prepared before the face of all peoples, a light to *bring* revelation to the Gentiles, and the glory of Your people Israel.'" Simeon was at the end of his life and God gave him the opportunity to be among the first to proclaim Jesus as the savior. Paul states in 2 Timothy 4:7–8: "I have fought the good fight, I have finished the race, I have kept the faith. Finally, there is laid up for me the crown of righteousness, which the Lord, the righteous Judge, will give to me on that Day, and not to me only but also to all who have loved His appearing." Don't you want to be among those that can say we've finished the race, we've kept the faith? Our greatest sense of purpose, when the days of our life have come to a close, will not come from the size of our bank account or the square footage of our homes but from the manner in which we have spread God's love to those around us. No matter what your life circumstances have been up to the present, may you use the time left to you in the pursuit of loving others the way God loved us. May that be your primary identity.

THE FINAL THING I'D LIKE TO SHARE IS A BREAKDOWN of the prayer used to close large groups in Celebrate Recovery. Other 12-step programs only use the first few lines, as it is a decidedly Christian prayer, but the principles outlined throughout the prayer are a great guide for living a Godly life. The prayer, written by *Reinhold Niebuhr in 1932, goes like this:*

> God grant me the serenity to accept the things I cannot change,
> courage to change the things I can, and the wisdom to know the difference, living one day at a time;
> enjoying one moment at a time;
> taking, as Jesus did, this sinful world as it is, not as I would have it;
> trusting that You will make all things right if I surrender to Your will;
> so that I may be reasonably happy in this life
> and supremely happy with You forever in the next. Amen.

The first request made to God is that we be granted serenity. I have been told that the root origin of the word "serenity" actually means "to see clearly." Think of how many problems in our life would be easier to accept if we were just able to see them clearly. By just acknowledging that what is, is, we can release much of our fear and anxiety and give it to the Lord. If you recognize you can't change a situation, is the anxiety really helping you? When Paul says he'd learned the secret to being content in any circumstance, I believe God had granted him the ability to accept any circumstance he was in. If I have a physical disability or a mental health diagnosis, I must accept that as a fact of life and operate according to God's will within that reality. If those around me have betrayed me or even abused me, I must accept that what has happened can't be undone and start on the road to healing. If there is news on television about chaos in the world that goes far beyond my capabilities, I need to accept my inability to control others and give this world to God. It is a freeing process to surrender those things we are powerless over and focus on those things within our abilities. If you are working with someone that is perpetuating their own suffering by raging against things beyond their control, this simple part of this simple prayer can be transformational. I heard an analogy of God standing beside us with a towel, wiping off our bloody head as we continue to bang it against a wall, trying to make a hole to go through. Every now and then He asks, "Are you ready to try the door yet?"

The next request is for the courage to change the things we can. There are few circumstances we can't respond to in some way, once we've accepted things as they are. We can't change how people mistreat us, but we can set appropriate boundaries. We can't change the weather, but we can buy an umbrella. We can't change all the chaos in the world around us, but we can be a voice of reason and an example of loving service to others. In my life, the times I neglected to do the right things were overwhelmingly not because I didn't know what to do, I was just too afraid or lazy to do it. I needed to be bold. It is possible to change long-held patterns of unhealthy behavior; they say, "Don't get hit by the same train twice." We can learn to get out of the way of the train. We can follow through on the difficult, positive action we've been putting off. 2 Timothy 1:7 states, "For God has not given us a spirit of fear, but of power and of love and of a sound mind." God can give us that kind of courage. All He needs from us is the follow-through.

The next request is for the wisdom to know the difference. There are many situations in life during which we aren't sure of the next right move. Should we accept things the way they are or work to change them? My wife and I were given the opportunity to move from Nebraska to Arizona about nine years ago. It was a difficult decision: I would be leaving a secure position with an employer I'd been with for fifteen years, we'd be moving to a small town in which I knew no one, and I'd be leaving behind a strong support network. After prayer and consultation with many people, as well as taking into account the steps of opportunity God presented to us, it became clear God wanted us to make the move. He didn't give us a postcard or speak from a burning bush, but in our quiet contemplation it became clear what His will was. I have learned that if God makes His will clear, its best to do what He asks. It didn't work out so well for Jonah when he didn't. We made the move and have been blessed with new friends, new support sources, and new opportunities to help others. Even though it hasn't been without challenges, I'm still confident this was God's will. I believe prayerful consideration of such dilemmas will usually result in a clear path. In helping others through such dilemmas, I believe it is more important to support their process of discovery than to make their decisions for them. The principle of wisdom is to be brave, but not foolish. Another important principle I've discovered is that God's will accounts for my mistakes. I'm not going to mess up so bad God thinks His will can't be done. Look at how many times the nation of Israel went against His will, and yet they achieved the task of bringing Christ into the world. Even their efforts to silence Jesus through His crucifixion brought about the necessary sacrifice for the forgiveness of our sins.

We want to always do what we believe is right, but even if we get it wrong, He can still work with us.

Living one day at a time is the next focus of the prayer. Though we tend to think of the concept of living one day at a time as modern, this prayer was actually written in the 1930s. The day we have right now is our only opportunity for action. Yesterday is beyond our ability to change, tomorrow is not available to us. I believe that if we can value the immeasurable worth of each moment of our life we will live in a constant state of grateful awe. In the Sermon on the Mount Jesus stated, "Therefore do not worry, saying, 'What shall we eat?' or 'What shall we drink?' or 'What shall we wear?' For after all these things the Gentiles seek. For your heavenly Father knows that you need all these things. But seek first the Kingdom of God and His righteousness, and all these things shall be added to you. Therefore, do not worry about tomorrow, for tomorrow will worry about its own things. Sufficient for the day *is* its own trouble." I've heard people say, "God won't give you more than you can handle in one day." I'd like to amend that to "God won't give you more than you and He can handle together." There are days I look up and say, "Boy, do You have a lot on your plate today." I am an advocate for to-do lists, as long as they include steps that are attainable in one day and include no more than seven items. I'm also an advocate of celebrating any small step forward, even if we can't complete everything we hoped to accomplish. There's the story of a man that went out on a beach where thousands of starfish were washed up. They would all die if they remained out of the water for long. The man began picking up starfish, one by one, and throwing them back in the sea. An onlooker commented,

"There's thousands of those starfish. What difference is it going to make to only throw a few of them back?" The man replied, as he was throwing one, "It made a difference to that one." Who knows what God can do with the small, positive actions we take in this day that He has given us?

Enjoying one moment at a time is a marvelous way to live. Life is supposed to be fun! When Paul says rejoice in the Lord always, that's not only permission but instruction to enjoy life in the moment. The caveat is "in the Lord." We can't expect to have lasting joy outside of His will. Look for the joy available in all the endeavors God leads you through and promote joy in others whenever possible.

Accepting hardship as the pathway to peace is the next focus of the prayer. The wax-on, wax-off lesson from the original *Karate Kid* movie is one of the most classic examples of hardship preparing us for future challenges. I heard a message from a high-ranking military officer about his basic training experience before serving in Vietnam. The assignment one day was to lie still for an extended period without making any movement. While this seemed pointless at the time, he tried to follow orders, until a bug crawled into his ear, driving him crazy. He slowly, very slowly, moved his arm up to his ear to get rid of the annoying bug. When he finally got his hand to his ear, he discovered his drill sergeant had been standing right behind him the whole time. As you can imagine, the sergeant had some choice things to say to him. Six months later he was in Vietnam, pinned down in the jungle with two others while an entire squadron of Vietcong passed by. He lay there, completely still, hoping the other two had the same strict training he had. The challenges we face today can lead to peaceful resolutions in the future.

Taking, as Jesus did, this sinful world as it is, not as I would have it, is a true challenge for most of us. Jesus spoke about the joys of the Kingdom of heaven and about the Devil being the great deceiver of this world. He said, "These things I have spoken to you, that in Me you may have peace. In the world you will have tribulation; but be of good cheer, I have overcome the world" (John 16:33). He understood the rampant sin in the world and understands the mixed-up world we now live in, but still says to be of good cheer because He has overcome it, through His sacrifice that insures our salvation. We don't need the world to change to have joy; all we need is to follow Him and hold fast to His promises.

Trusting that You will make all things right can also be a challenge. I heard a great interview with Rick Warren, author of *The Purpose Driven Life* and co-founder of Celebrate Recovery, that gave clarity to the idea of "all things right." He described formerly thinking that life was a series of hills and valleys; some days you're up, some days you're down. After his wife experienced serious health problems at about the same time the book became wildly successful, he changed his view. He now sees life as two train tracks going side by side; at any time you have personal struggles, big or small, that you can choose to focus on, as well as plenty of things you can choose to be grateful for. The reason for this: God is more interested in our character than in our comfort. All things right does not equate with all things being easy or safe; all things right means it will all lead to fulfillment of His will if we strive to be guided by Him.

If I surrender to His will is the qualifier. Surrender has been looked down on in the modern world. Yet surrender to God's will is the primary goal of the 12 steps and often indicated in scripture, including the direct instruction in James 4:7—"Therefore submit to God. Resist the devil and he will flee from you." I have been told by lifeguards that it is difficult to save a person from drowning until they are done fighting to survive. If a lifesaver tries to rescue a person flailing about, they may both drown. The person in need has to submit before they can be saved.

The final thought in the prayer "so that I may be reasonably happy in this life and supremely happy with You forever in the next" is the ultimate comforting hope all Christians have. I would review this prayer in a group periodically while working in secular counseling settings. I would say, "If you do not believe in a life after this one, I am extremely limited in my ability to encourage you." I have complete faith in the afterlife and in Jesus's promise that those who believe in Him by obeying His Gospel will have salvation in heaven. I also believe that a life lived by Godly principles leads to the greatest chance of present happiness, but even if we do face trials, they "are not worthy to be compared with the glory which shall be revealed in us" (Romans 8:18).

I hope I have been able to equip you with some tools that can help you in aiding those you encounter through their emotional and spiritual struggles. I pray you may stay motivated to serve at every opportunity God gives you and will seek the aid of others when you yourself are in need. May God bless you as you do so.

Pope-isms

I have used a wide range of slogans, quips, and sayings over the decades to help people through their struggles. A coworker dubbed them "Pope-isms," though very few of them actually originated with me. I have been encouraged by several people to collect them into a list, so here goes, with sources indicated as I could find them. Many are scattered throughout the book; many are added to help you in your efforts to help others.

> If you always do what you always did, you'll always get what you always got. —Henry Ford
>
> Try not. Do or do not. There is no try. —Yoda in *The Empire Strikes Back*
>
> Stupidity should be painful. —Unknown
>
> You can catch more flies with honey than you can with vinegar. —Benjamin Franklin
>
> Many people fail because they have no goal beyond success. —Scott Somerville
>
> Don't outrun your headlights. —Recovery slogan
>
> No one cares how much you know until they know how much you care. —Teddy Roosevelt
>
> The main thing is to keep the main thing the main thing. —Stephen Covey
>
> Easy does it, but do it. —A.A. slogan

Don't quit before the miracle happens. —A.A. slogan

SLIP=Serious Lapse In Program. —N.A. slogan

You're just one pebble on a great big beach. You're just as valuable as all the other pebbles, but it ain't your beach. —David J. Pope

Be the person your dog thinks you are. —J.W. Stephens

An addict alone is in bad company. —N.A. Slogan

Relapse is not a part of recovery, it's a part of addiction. —David J. Pope

You can't heal a wound by pretending it's not there. —NLT translation of Jeremiah 6:14

Don't should on yourself. —Keith Ellis, PhD

Bloom where you are planted. —St. Francis de Sales

Falling isn't a sign of failure. Not getting up is. —Paraphrased from Mary Pickford

If one person tells you that you have a tail, they're probably crazy. If twelve people in a row tell you that you have a tail, look behind you. —Paraphrased from Jack Rosenblum

Let go and let God. —A.A. slogan

Not my circus, not my monkeys. —Unknown

This too shall pass. —A.A. slogan

Wherever you go, there you are. —Jim Russell

It is better to travel hopefully than to arrive. —Robert Lewis Stevenson

Unsolicited advice is criticism. — Dr. Ross Campbell

When you come to the end of your rope, let go. —Geoffrey Rose

Treat your mind like a bad neighborhood—don't go in there alone. —Paraphrase from Anne Lamott

If it ain't broke, don't fix it. —T. Bert Lance

Direction, not intention, determines your destination. —Andy Stanley

The good is often the enemy of the best. —Edwin Louis Cole

You're either working on your recovery or you're working on a relapse. —Recovery slogan

We came, we came to, we came to believe. —Recovery slogan

GRACE=God's Redemption At Christ's Expense. —Unknown

A journey of a thousand miles begins with the first step. —Lao Tzu

Nothing changes until it becomes real. —Terry Kellog

God never wastes a hurt. —Celebrate Recovery slogan

Don't quit before the miracle happens. —Recovery slogan

Hurt people tend to hurt people. —Celebrate Recovery slogan

It's easier to act your way into feeling better than to feel your way into acting better. —Attributed to several sources

If you feel far away from God, guess who moved. —Robin Jones Gunn

If you walk away from God, the path back is always one step, because He's right behind you the whole time. —Unknown

DETACH=Don't Even Think About Controlling Him/her. —Al-anon acronym

LOVE=Let Others Voluntarily Evolve. —Al-anon acronym

What would be the right thing to do if I didn't feel this way? —Recovery slogan

A problem accurately diagnosed is 85 percent solved. —Paraphrase from Charles Kettering

Resentment is like drinking poison hoping the other person will die. —Quoted by several, including Carrie Fisher and Nelson Mandela

Life has two rules: 1) Don't sweat the small stuff, 2) It's all small stuff. —From the book by Richard Carlson

Believe you can, believe you can't; either way you're right. —Paraphrased from Henry Ford

There are no great people in this world, only great challenges which ordinary people rise to meet. —William Frederick Halsey, Jr.

Great leaders don't produce good followers, they produce new leaders. —Tom Peters

Recovery is a process, not an event. —Recovery slogan

Practice makes progress toward perfection. —Unknown

I'm one of "those people." —Celebrate Recovery slogan

HALTS = Don't get too Hungry, Angry Lonely, Tired, or Stressed. —Recovery slogan

Marriage is not 50/50; its 100/100. —Unknown

Coincidence is God's way of remaining anonymous. —Albert Einstein

Live each day as if it were your last. Someday it will be. —Paraphrase from Malachy McCourt

A.A. is not a self-help program, it is a help others program. —From an A.A. leader

If you want a happy spouse, be the spouse that would make your spouse happy. —Unknown

The truth doesn't change because of what people say, think or do. —Adapted from a Booker T. Washington quote

How do you eat an elephant? One bite at a time. —Desmond Tutu

Behold the turtle that makes progress only when he sticks his neck out. —James B. Conant

Preach the Gospel at all times; when necessary, use words. —Francis of Assisi

Struggles grow in the dark and shrink in the light of day. —Unknown

God won't give you more than you and He can handle together. —Unknown

Do the next right thing. —Attributed to multiple sources

You can't keep what you have unless you give it away. —Recovery slogan

You can't save your soul and your face at the same time. —Adapted from a Lyndon Johnson quote

If God doesn't have your attention, He'll get a bigger hammer. —David J. Pope

Can prayer help with a toothache? Yes, if said on the way to the dentist's office. —Joseph Martin

Instead of telling God how big your troubles are, try telling your troubles how big your God is. —Joel Osteen

A friend is someone who, when you make a fool of yourself, doesn't think you've done a permanent job. —Laurence J. Peter

Don't get hit by the same train twice. —Unknown

Acknowledgments

I'd like to thank the many people that encouraged me to write this book and contributed their experiences, including my wife Paula, my daughter Rachelle, Dale, Alan, Tony, Bill, Vin, Becky, Julie, and John. I'd also like to thank the hundreds of people I had the honor of serving as a therapist, sponsor, or accountability partner.

References

Anonymous Contributors. Alcoholics Anonymous Big Book, 4th ed. 2002. Alcoholics Anonymous.

American Psychiatric Association. *Diagnostic and Statistical Manual of Mental Health Disorders, 5th Edition: DSM-5 TR.* 2022. American Psychiatric Association Publishing.

Harley, Willard F. Jr. *His Needs, Her Needs: Building an Affair-Proof Marriage.* 2011. Revell.

Harris, Joshua. *I Kissed Dating Goodbye: A New Attitude Toward Relationships and Romance.* 2003. Multnomah Books.

Howard, Ron, director. *A Beautiful Mind.* Universal Pictures. 2001.

Kubler-Ross, Elisabeth. *On Death and Dying.* 1969. Collier Books/MacMillan Publishing.

Lewis, C. S. *The Problem of Pain.* Paperback published 2015. Harper One.

McAuliffe, Mary Boesen and Robert Michael. *The Essentials of Chemical Dependency.* 1975. American Chemical Dependency Assoc. World Services.

McDowell, Josh. *More Than a Carpenter.* 1987. Living Books.

Pelzer, Dave. *A Child Called It: One Child's Courage to Survive.* 1995. Health Communications, Inc.

Stein, Michael, PsD. "Thoughts Are Just Thoughts: How to Stop Worshiping Your Anxious Mind." https://adaa.org/learn-from-us/from-the-experts/blog-posts/consumer/thoughts-are-just-thoughts.

Strobel, Lee. *The Case For Christ*. 2016. Zondervan Books.

Wallace, Warner. *Cold Case Christianity: A Homicide Detective Investigates the Claims of the Gospels*. 2013. David C. Cook Publisher.

ONLINE SOURCES

Al-anon information can be obtained from www.al-anon.org.

Celebrate Recovery information can be obtained from www.celebraterecovery.com.

DivorceCare information can be obtained from www.divorcecare.org.

EMDR information can be obtained from www.emdr.com.

GriefShare information can be obtained from www.griefshare.org.

NAMI information can be obtained from www.nami.org.

About the Author

David J. Pope has Master's degrees in Human Relations and Christian Counseling. He has worked as a licensed mental health/addiction therapist in Nebraska, Iowa and Arizona over the course of a forty-year career. He lives in Northern Arizona with his wife (her story is in chapter 11).

www.ingramcontent.com/pod-product-compliance
Lightning Source LLC
LaVergne TN
LVHW021824060526
838201LV00058B/3500